To:
Scott

May you be
your own hero

Roger Bear

In the Hearts of Peaceful Heroes:
Their Shared and Inspiring Values

Roger F. Cram

For fifteen years, I taught and researched at four Northeast Ohio colleges the inspiring and compassionate leadership skills repeatedly utilized by my eighty, hand-picked, world heroes of peace. I was probing among them for any commonly shared values and skills of compassion that I could embody into my character. I discovered fourteen of them. They have enriched my life beyond my comprehension. I now wish to share them with you.

—Roger F. Cram

In the Hearts of Peaceful Heroes by Roger Cram is part history, memoir, and how-to-guide. Incredible stories illuminate the extraordinary lives of peaceful heroes from around the globe. Using research, interviews, and personal experience, Cram has unearthed hundreds of rarely heard stories and anecdotes from people who faced extraordinary obstacles yet maintained their dignity, character, and values. Every word about the Tuskegee Airmen is a must-read for every American. Along the way, Cram's reflections and insights add humor and wisdom to your reading experience. Looking for a way to live and love in the world? I fully recommend this book!

—Rev. Chad Delaney
Senior Pastor, Mantua Center Christian Church

Somebody must keep paying the price for freedom. That is what becoming a hero of peace involves, not just in the military, but in civilian life as well. Heroes of peace become aware of critical situations and have the ability, confidence, and the willingness to intervene. *In the Hearts of Peaceful Heroes* offers researched and discovered heroic values of peace and presents them as a self-embodying opportunity.

—Lt Col Alexander Jefferson, USAF, Retired
Tuskegee Airmen P-51 Redtail Fighter Pilot
Author: *Red Tail Captured, Red Tail Free*
Prisoner of War, Germany, WWII

Roger Cram's depth of wisdom jumps out at you from his first written words. I find his subject matter and writing match his wit, zeal for life, and zest for knowledge of "spirit." He brings "Hero Values" to light in layman terms. Roger has an innate ability to express hilarious experiences (humor at his expense sometimes) to heart-wrenching accounts of witnesses in the same breath. He is thirsty for understanding. Roger Cram is a TEACHER!

—Rose E. Grier Evans
Artist/Writer/Victim Advocate

In the Hearts of Peaceful Heroes:
Their Shared and Inspiring Values
By Roger F. Cram
www.hiramwestpublishing@gmail.com

Published by Hiram West Publishing, LLC
6752 Bancroft St. P.O. Box 642, Hiram, Ohio 44234-0642

Editors
Editor-in-Chief: Carol Donley Ph.D.,
Emerita Professor of English, Hiram College
Managing Editor: G. M. Donley
Guest Editor: Janice DiMichele, Jan Joyce and Assoc. Lyndhurst, Ohio
Guest Editor: Reverend Chad Delaney, Mantua Center Christian Church
Guest Editor: Rose E. Grier Evans. Artist/Writer/Victim Advocate

Cover and interior design: G. M. Donley

Photographs are by Roger F. Cram or used by permission
or in the public domain unless noted

Foreword and Consultant: Dr. Andrew Hoffman, Ph.D.
Innovative Psychologist

ISBN: 979-8-9860431-0-4 (print)
Printed in USA

Library of Congress Control Number: 2022917746

First Edition November 2022

Table of Contents

Dedication   1

Foreword   2

Preface   3

Acknowledgments   6

Introduction   7

Chapter 1

Discovering the Values of Heroes of Peace   9

   I.   The Events that Kindled My Research into   10
World Heroes of Peace

   II. The Tuskegee Airmen: A Brief History—   27
Discovering their Values

   III. How I Came to Know and Admire the Tuskegee Airmen   73

Chapter 2

The Values of Behavior, Creating Change, and Recognizing   83
Achievements of Others

   • Nelson Mandela: My Greatest Hero of Peace   86

   • Paul Harris: Created the World's Largest Society   96
of Compassion **RI***

   • Principal Daniels' Elementary School: Turns Criminals into   100
Angels **RI***

Chapter 3

The Values of Developing Vision and Overcoming Obstacles   107

   • Hannah Taylor: A Child Caring for the Homeless **RI***   109

   • Ryan Hreljac: A Canadian Child Caring for Poor Uganda   112
Children **RI***

   • Efran Pennaflorida: A Child Educating Slum Children   113

Chapter 4

The Values of Sustaining Self-Esteem and   117
Showing Compassion

   • Hal Reichle: The Hero of Anonymous Giving   119

   • Glenys van Halter: Rescuing Children from their Abusers   132

RI* denotes people or projects involving Rotary International

- The Claw Lady: Enchantress of Khayelitsha, South Africa–   140
  Rescuing New Orphans
- Flower Man: The Poor Caring for the Poor **RI***   143

Chapter 5
The Values of Addressing Courage and Perseverance   147
- Irena Sendler: Rescuing Jewish Infants Under the Nazis' Eyes   149
- Masalakulangwa Mabula: A Former Street Child Returns   153
  to the streets **RI***
- Reverend Corine McClintoc: The Magic of Sparrow Village **RI***   156
- Dr. Meena Patel: The Angel of Problem Solving **RI***   164

Chapter 6
The Values of Encouraging Trust, Managing Conflict,   171
Preserving Character, and Revering these Values
- Gilbert Doho: Fights for Women's Rights by Stealth and   173
  Incognito
- Olga Sanchez: Rescues Victims of the Beast **RI***   177
- John Robert Lewis: Courage Beyond Comprehension   180
- Father Marco Dessy and Frank Huezo: 186
  Amigos of Compassion **RI***

Appendix   201
- The Tuskegee Airmen speeches and programs
  given by Roger Cram
- How many American bombers were shot down by German
  fighters?
- The shared characteristics of peace from my eighty selected
  heroes
- My eighty selected heroes of peace

RI* denotes people or projects involving Rotary International

Dedication

I dedicate this book to you, the reader, as I invite you to vicariously join me on a wonderful and inspiring journey into the hearts and minds of world heroes of peace. Accompany me in this book as I interview world heroes of peace and explore their wonderful histories. Travel with me into the ghettos of South Africa and the mountain villages of Nicaragua looking for heroes among the destitute. You will be amazed at the heroes we will find. Let's start walking together. Wear comfortable shoes.

Foreword

By Dr. Andrew Hoffman, Ph.D.—Innovative Psychologist—Advisor for this book

Often a foreword claims that readers will not be able to put the book down because they are so eager to find out what happens. However, I claim that readers will often put this book down, not because they are bored, but because they want time to think about the challenging ideas in these pages. Some of these stories of heroic behavior may be familiar to readers; others are being told for the first time. What is new in every case are different perspectives about what the stories mean and the discovery of what they have in common.

So, expect to be surprised—to acknowledge that you may never have thought about it this way before or realized what connects heroic behavior in different times, places, and cultures.

Roger Cram has discovered 14 values that his heroes embodied as they worked towards their goals, and he identifies their common ways of dealing with problems. For example, if his heroes met with violence, they remained calm; if they encountered angry outbursts, they stayed quiet.

They reacted kindly and peacefully to hostile aggression.

Cram posits that his heroes learned how to react calmly to negative situations. Some of his best examples involve the Tuskegee Airmen, who proved that black men could be heroic fighter pilots although the American military asserted they were too ignorant to learn how to fly.

So, some aspects of this book are essentially a memoir of his experiences studying his Heroes and discovering their values. Other aspects are the social histories of his selected heroes as they acted in their cultural/political contexts. And some of the book offers guidance for readers as to how to make themselves more like the heroes they admire. Cram says, "How you react to what happens to you is who you are—for everyone to see."

I know you will find a great deal to ponder.

Preface

Roger F. Cram

This book is an in-depth study of how heroes of peace use compassion in the face of adversity. It is the research of how special heroes successfully address hatred with peace, how their calmness softens the chaos surrounding them, and why they always maintain the dignity of their adversaries throughout their enemies' defeat and recovery. Heroes of peace typically react to a crisis with positive and compassionate characteristics—that is one of the credentials that makes them heroes of peace.

This book is rich in heroic stories based on little-known sources of information discovered through my research. For example, an inspirational letter sent from a combat pilot to his mother after a fearsome air battle in WWII, incarcerated freedom fighters secretly confronting brutal dictators from their prison cells, and a child—who launched from his elementary school classroom—a compassionate humanitarian campaign that saved thousands of lives. I obtained more unknown information from personal interviews with many heroes of peace, from a heroic survivor of a liberation army in Nicaragua, from a prior child soldier in Cameroon, and from a revolutionary who fought the suppressive Apartheid government in South Africa. These incredible quests are true, often appearing surreal, and interlace this book with unbelievable ventures rarely found in any media other than from the personal exploits of the heroes themselves. The inspiring values these heroes employed to succeed in their noble pursuits are most remarkable.

I researched, discovered, and taught these heroic values in college courses for over a decade, and my students and I studied extensively the inspiring values used by magnificent people to guide their critical decisions. We studied these heroes only when they were performing at their best. No human being is perfect and without flaws. No person can go through life without committing careless errors. Gandhi had bad days.

Please understand this book is not a study of perfect heroes of peace—there are none. This book is a study of the values and thought processes of (a) magnificent world heroes of peace (b) when they were performing at their best—what wonderful and proven examples of outstanding human conduct to study.

I was interested in HOW heroes of peace achieved their remarkable deeds instead of what they accomplished. Where could I find such world heroes of peace to study? How could I interact with enough of them and long enough to learn the values in their hearts?

Into my life came the Tuskegee Airmen

I started my journey in 2002 by first researching the heroic Tuskegee Airmen, a group of young black men and women who served as pilots and support staff for the U.S. Army Air Corps in WWII. At that point, the U.S. military used blacks only as mess cooks, laborers, and janitors. They were not allowed to be pilots. A program was started by President Roosevelt to see if blacks could be trained to fly military aircraft; thus, a flight school for blacks was started in Tuskegee, Alabama. This positive goal was deliberately undermined by many whites in authority (Southern senators, congressman, military officers) to show that blacks did NOT possess the intelligence, courage, or ability to efficiently fly or maintain military aircraft. However, despite cruel discrimination, inferior equipment, unreasonable standards, restricted rights, limited privileges, and insufficient support, the Tuskegee Airmen and Women succeeded with unprecedented achievements still unmatched today. How did they do this? How did their values prevail undaunted among the corruption and prejudice of their leaders? How did their confidence, effectiveness, ambition, and self-esteem remain intact among degrading discrimination and cruel treatment from their supervisors? How did they maintain their high ethics and loyalty to the United States when this country considered them incompetent to defend it?

Key Point

The Tuskegee Airmen fought against Germany to keep Hitler from developing his "superior race," while their own country, the United States, treated them like a subhuman species. The Tuskegee Airmen defended and died for a country that would often not allow them to use a public drinking fountain. What inspired the Airmen to fight for this country? How did they do this? I had to find out.

Other heroes of peace around the world

While I was researching the Tuskegee Airmen, I expanded my project and studied well-known heroes like Nelson Mandela, Mahatma Gandhi, John Robert Lewis, and Mother Teresa. I also traveled over seven years and walked with unknown heroes living in poverty throughout the townships in South Africa and the poor mountain villages in Nicaragua. The heroes of peace I found dwelling amid the impoverished were indeed inspiring. They treated the indigent with dignity, the disrespectful with respect. They performed with excellence for those believing them incompetent and formed an alliance of peace and respect for those plotting their failure.

I did discover a commonality among the crisis-management methodologies and values of the inspiring world heroes I researched. There IS an effective and peaceful means of managing a crisis calmly. This, to me, is awe-inspiring.

Let no one ever come to you without leaving better and happier.
Mother Teresa

Falling down is an accident. Staying down is a choice.
Unknown

Acknowledgments

I gratefully thank all the special individuals below who through their efforts and selfless dedication of their time and knowledge made this book possible.

The Tuskegee Airmen, their history, their legacy, their courage, and their inner peace. A fifteen-year study and personal relationship with over fifty of the Tuskegee Airmen and Women made this book possible.

Carol Ruggie, my co-researcher for this book, died of pancreatic cancer before this book was finished. Her love and compassion for children in crises were awe-inspiring. She felt the heroes' values presented in this book are critical to the future success of our children and our world.

Dr. Andrew Hoffman, Ph.D. Innovative psychologist, who supported and encouraged this book by serving as a guide substantiating many of the psychological materials and recommending additional resources for authentication.

Carol Donley, Ph.D., my sister, professor of English at Hiram College in Hiram, Ohio, who faithfully served for fifteen years as one of my advisors and editors.

Robin Jean Patzel, my daughter, who spent hours interviewing many Tuskegee Women creating a verbal history of their heroic behavior.

More than 1,000 students at Hiram College who attended my classes and aided me with my research involving heroes of peace. Hundreds of comparison-contrast essays were submitted researching the values of world heroes of peace.

Dr. Jack Soules, author of *The Curse of Being Human*, opened my eyes to human-instinctual behavior and how most of man's detrimental conduct is ingrained in our brains from birth. Realizing this gives us an opportunity to correct and overcome these negative inclinations opening our life to unlimited positive opportunities.

Hal Reichle, a wonderfully mysterious and enchanting man, probably changed my life more than any other person. Hal, who spent his life secretly giving to total strangers, was killed while piloting a helicopter in the first Gulf war called Desert Storm. The amazing legacy Hal has left this world, and the opportunity he offers you, the reader of this book, will be enriching forever.

Introduction

Where can we view multiple examples of just how magnificent a human being can become?

This book will present the ability heroes of peace have to inspire positive change, not through criticism, but through continuous achievements and examples of excellence for all to witness. You will learn how heroes of peace honor their commitments and obligations to everyone, for their pledge is as meaningful to a king as to a beggar. They know that they must decide how to behave, and that choice must be based on their values, never on how others behave toward them.

We learn far more from our mistakes and failures than we learn from our successes. A person who has failed many times has an incredible knowledge base, which might be more valuable than a person who has been more successful. Abraham Lincoln was born into poverty, lost eight elections, failed twice in business, and had a total nervous breakdown—all before he was elected President of the United States.[1] Franklin D. Roosevelt flunked out of Columbia Law School. Dwight D. Eisenhower was rejected for his first three positions of command. Harry Truman went bankrupt after his first two years of managing a shirt and hat shop. Does this mean that all these impressive gentlemen were losers or prone to failure? Of course not. One of the first acts Lincoln did after the Civil War was to make sure all the captured spoils of war—wagons, horses, firearms, etc.—were returned to the Confederate soldiers so they could continue working, farming, and supporting their families after the war. This is an example of leading with compassion. World heroes of peace do not let what they can't do keep them from doing what they can do.

---

1 Abraham Lincoln and Failure, Snopes.com, https://www.snopes.com>fact-check>Glurge Gallery

---

Key Point

There are many other ways of addressing problems than those caring ways utilized by heroes of peace. This book is not intended to offer the way all humans should always behave; it is not intended as a panacea of perfect human conduct. This book offers the values and methodologies repeatedly used by world heroes of peace to calmly solve problems. Therefore, the compassionate techniques presented in this book have been successfully used thousands of times by multitudes of peaceful heroes for centuries. I would say these are reliably proven practices. They are eye-opening, empowering, transforming, and very timely in our troubled society.

Life always offers you a second chance; it's called tomorrow.
Unknown

A person who never made a mistake never tried anything new.
Albert Einstein

Chapter One

Discovering the Values of Heroes of Peace

In three parts:
I. The Events that Kindled my Research
II. The Tuskegee Airmen
III. How I Came to Know and Admire the Airmen

*There is a perpetual battle in your heart between Good and Evil.
Which one will win this conflict? The one you feed!*
Native American, Wampanoag Tribe, Western U.S.

How far you go in life depends on you being tender with the young, compassionate with the aged, sympathetic with the striving, and tolerant of the weak and the strong. Because someday in life you will have been all of these.
George Washington Carver

If what you accomplished during your previous hour only benefited you, you shouldn't have done it. If what you intend to accomplish during your next hour only benefits you, don't do it.
Gilbert Doho, Professor Emeritus, Case Western Reserve University, Cleveland, Ohio

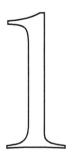

I. The Events that Kindled My Research into World Heroes of Peace

Many times I am provided with unique opportunities having the potential to enrich my life beyond my dreams. This happens to all of us. I often do not recognize these occasions—some unusual event, a suddenly realized insight, an off-the-cuff inspirational comment, or the awareness of an unfulfilled need may beckon my attention.

A TV movie titled "The Tuskegee Airmen" so motivated me that I spent the next fifteen years developing a teaching method to convey the Tuskegee Airmen's remarkable control and compassion for themselves and others. These heroes' insights will hopefully inspire and enrich you with their wisdom and compassion as they did me.

How my inspiring adventures all began

On a lazy Sunday afternoon in August of 1996, I was watching television. The movie "The Tuskegee Airmen" was starting. "Never heard of them." I said to myself. "Must be a movie about Native Americans," I thought. The name Tuskegee sounded to me to have an American Indian origin, but I noticed several black men in the movie. "What do they have to do with Tuskegee Indians?" I wondered. "What kind of movie is this?"

My curiosity for this movie caused me to pay closer attention. Halfway through I was sitting on the edge of the couch. The last ten minutes I was standing up, cheering, for what the Tuskegee Airmen had accomplished in the movie was almost impossible. I felt a little silly standing up in my house, alone, and applauding a television movie, but I could not believe what I was seeing. Then I realized this movie could not possibly be true. It was obviously a larger-than-life adventure movie like "Raiders of the Lost Ark," "Gladiator," or some of the 007 spy thriller escapades. I relaxed realizing the movie was just a tall tale. "Good show," I thought. I was glad I saw the movie.

Two weeks later I attended the Cleveland, Ohio, Air Show at Burke Lake Front Airport. Because I am a pilot and flight instructor, I was paying particular attention to all the aircraft displays and aerial acrobatics demonstrations. The announcer then said something that left me stunned. "All of you who want to meet the original Tuskegee Airmen, they have a booth at the end of the field. Go on down there and thank them for their service to this country. Don't forget to get an autograph!"

I felt like I was a six-year-old boy who was just told Peter Pan was real and waiting to talk to me! Have you ever seen the cartoon when the Road Runner is standing still, then suddenly, he is not there being replaced by a puff of smoke and a high zing sound? That is what happened to me. I was gone. Puff! The next thing I knew my feet were running toward the end of the field. I do not remember telling them to do that, they just took off on their own. My mind gradually caught up to my legs chanting "Feet, don't fail me now." I had never run that fast for over half a mile before. I was fifty-seven years old, overweight, out of shape, and within five minutes found myself standing in front of five, distinguished, elderly, gentlemen all wearing Tuskegee Airmen caps. I could not speak, but simply stared at five original Tuskegee Airmen, larger-than-life, sitting before me signing autographs. My mind raced back to the Tuskegee Airmen movie and all those unbelievable accomplishments—could they really be true?

At the Tuskegee Airmen's booth, I met Dr. Jack Soules. He was a Caucasian volunteer working with the Tuskegee Airmen and gave me my initial introduction into their incredible accomplishments. The name Dr. Jack Soules might sound familiar to you. He wrote *The Curse of Being Human*, one of my reference sources listed in the Acknowledgments section of this book. Dr. Jack Soules was a Professor Emeritus at Cleveland State University. His remarkable book helps explain our human behavior and why we are so aggressive.

I spent the next two hours at the Tuskegee Airmen booth talking with Dr. Jack Soules, learning about many of the Tuskegee Airmen's nearly impossible accomplishments. Most were done under adverse conditions, and all were true.

The air show was over

As I was driving home from the Cleveland Air Show, I was inspired, happy, and filled with excitement. My mind was racing in a thousand directions, but the more I drove, the more anger developed in me. How could my mood turn from exhilaration to anger with no explanation? What was happening to me? I began to realize that I felt cheated! I felt deprived! I felt short changed! I was 57 years old and had not heard of these magnificent Tuskegee Airmen before. I had gone to exceptionally good schools, but the Tuskegee Airmen were not in my history books. They were nowhere to be found in my social studies texts. What is going on?

I thought perhaps the Tuskegee Airmen were better known to blacks than whites, so I stopped at the Shell gas station at East 30th St. in Cleveland. I met the black store owner outside. I said to him in an excited voice, "I just left the Cleveland Air Show, and some original Tuskegee Airmen are giving out autographs."

He replied, "Who are the Tuskegee Airmen?" Not believing his statement, I ran into the convenience store and up to a clerk at the register.

"I just left the Cleveland Air Show and there are some original Tuskegee Airmen giving autographs." I excitedly announced.

"Who are the Tuskegee Airmen?" she inquired.

I was very confused. How could such magnificent people like the Tuskegee Airmen, who have sacrificed for this country in so many ways, be unknown—especially to blacks? I never heard of them before I saw the movie. The Shell gas station owner never heard of them. The cash register clerk never heard of them. Something was very wrong.

I was later to learn that the Tuskegee Airmen were kept a secret to protect the egos of white southern politicians and military supervisors. No southern white politician was going to allow blacks to be recognized as intelligent, compassionate, and highly capable war heroes. This was especially true after these same politicians and military officers were so vocal about the black man's lack of intelligence required to fly aircraft.

To hide the incredible accomplishments of the Tuskegee Airmen, the government only paid white newspaper reporters to go to white military bases. The Tuskegee Airmen military bases were segregated and kept a secret. To maintain the secrecy of the Tuskegee Airmen's accomplishments, their war records were locked up (sequestered) for twenty-five years after the war.[2]

I brought the Tuskegee Airmen to Hiram College

I set up a seminar at Hiram College about the Tuskegee Airmen and invited 250 high school students from Cleveland to attend. On that memorable day, five yellow school buses all arrived in front of Hiram College's auditorium. As the buses unloaded, I led 250 kids into the theater. It was packed. I stood on the auditorium stage and asked all these vibrant children, "Before today, how many of you have heard about the Tuskegee Airmen?" Only two students raised their hands.

I showed these students the HBO movie "The Tuskegee Airmen" after talking to them for about fifteen minutes describing what they were going

---

2 Told to the author in a personal interview with Mrs. Edith Roberts, Tuskegee trained pilot, and wife of the first original Tuskegee Airmen George Spencer Roberts, first graduating class from the Tuskegee Airmen flying program, 2010.

to see. After the movie, I went back up on the auditorium stage. I noticed immediately that the mood had changed in these students. They were angry. I asked several students why they seemed so upset after watching such an inspiring movie? They said to me:

> For years you white folks have been demanding that we blacks try harder to get along with you, but you whites never told us how to do this. Here, in the movie we just saw, the Tuskegee Airmen showed us how. The secrets about getting along with whites, or blacks, or with anybody for that matter, was demonstrated and understood by these blacks, the Tuskegee Airmen, not the whites. The Tuskegee Airmen are our heroes too, black heroes for black kids, yet they were kept a secret from us. Why?

The kids felt cheated. They felt short changed. They had never heard of the magnificent Tuskegee Airmen before. The Tuskegee Airmen were not in the kid's history books. They were nowhere to be found in the kid's social studies texts. What's going on?

The 250 inner-city kids felt exactly as I did when I first learned about the Airmen—cheated by our educational system. When they showed me their anger after seeing the *Tuskegee Airmen* movie, I felt my angry feelings driving home from the Cleveland Air Show were validated. In fact, when the Tuskegee Airmen's records were sequestered, every citizen of the United States had been cheated.

Having lunch with the Tuskegee Airmen

I then made a big mistake. I told the kids that I had a surprise for them. I left the stage and went to the back of the auditorium by the entrance door. I then turned and shouted, "You kids know you are about to have lunch, right?"

"Yes!" came a unison shout from the group.

"Well," I shouted back, "Your lunch is waiting for you in the building across the street called the Kennedy Center. The surprise is that there are five original Tuskegee Airmen waiting there to have lunch with you."

Why did I call this a mistake? Because I was standing in the exit door at the time and was nearly trampled as a stampede of 250 kids, all wide-eyed, shouting, and running—they barely left me with my life!

The luncheon with the inner-city kids and the Tuskegee Airmen went wonderfully. I introduced to the kids the original Tuskegee Airmen who were kind enough to come to Hiram College for this program. Original

Tuskegee Airman Tommy Austin, Arthur Saunders, Roy Richardson, Clarence Jamison, and James Travis were present. The Airmen loved interacting with the kids and answered as many of their questions as they could. The president of Hiram College stopped by and gave a welcome speech. I then interviewed some of the kids. I was very anxious to see if they were as excited as I was about the Tuskegee Airmen. I quickly found many were. One of the kids said he now knew what he wanted to do with his life. He wanted to be a history teacher and teach his students what they needed to know, like the Tuskegee Airmen for example, and other areas where his education had been shortchanged.

The Hiram College Tuskegee Airmen course became a reality

I desperately wanted to teach the students at Hiram College about the heroic determination and accomplishments of the Tuskegee Airmen. After eighteen months of work, my Tuskegee Airmen college course was finally approved by the New Course Committee and adopted into the Hiram College course catalog.

One of the main purposes of creating and teaching my course was to research the Tuskegee Airmen and see if I could discover HOW they accomplished their nearly impossible tasks. I really did not believe I would find a pattern, a set of values, or a common methodology used by most of the Airmen as a basis for their peaceful decisions while in a crisis. However, the prospect was so captivating that its possibility drove me forward with great determination.

Instead of deciding what heroic values I wanted to find, I felt it would be much more productive to study the accomplishments of the Tuskegee Airmen and see what heroic values they were displaying. As I studied the Tuskegee Airmen's accomplishments over the years, I noticed fourteen frequently repeated behavior characteristics that were quite wonderful, promoted trust, and were effective for peaceful negotiations in a crisis. These positive behavior characteristics captured my attention. However, I was very confused. How do such inspiring values of peace come from trained combatants of war? How were these values presented and practiced by so many of the Tuskegee Airmen originating from all over the United States? Where did they learn the extraordinary application of these values to peacefully solve their crisis problems? Did they know what their values were or were they ingrained in them from their upbringing?

After one year of researching the Tuskegee Airmen's accomplishments and behavior choices, and after consulting with my first-year students, the heroic values we felt were the most remarkable, the ones that resulted in the most positive outcomes, and the ones that repeatedly resolved a crisis peacefully for the Airmen, were as follows:

1. Controlling one's **behavior** in abusive situations
2. Creating positive **change** without using criticism
3. Developing positive **vision** among negativities
4. Overcoming **obstacles** enthusiastically
5. Maintaining **self-esteem** during discrimination and prejudice
6. Displaying **compassion** in the face of hostility
7. Respecting **fear** for only fear requires courage
8. Maintaining **persistence** with difficult goals
9. **Trusting** without justification
10. Managing **conflict** peacefully
11. **Reacting positively** to negativity
12. **Judging** no one
13. **Recognizing others'** triumphs
14. **Revering** these values

My students and I discovered these 14 values repeatedly used by the Tuskegee Airmen to resolve their ever-present crises. I also located seventy-nine other world heroes of peace that used the same fourteen values to resolve their problems peacefully. How could this be? What a remarkable discovery!

Key Point

These above values do not appear revolutionary. For example, trust, compassion, and reacting positively are common values used by good people everywhere. They certainly are not great insights resulting from years of research. However, my discovery is not the names of the values, but how these heroes of peace applied them to peacefully resolve a crisis, what actions they took to bring these ideals into fruition. This will become apparent as you continue reading.

For the first few years, my students and I interviewed Tuskegee Airmen and Women and wrote essays about their accomplishments in the face of prejudice and discrimination. Each year, the Tuskegee Airmen National

Convention was held in a different location in the United States. I attended the convention in Orlando, Omaha, Las Vegas, and Philadelphia as did some of my students. We interviewed more than one hundred Airmen researching their feelings about all the mistreatment they suffered through and the lack of recognition for their incredible achievements. I became friends with many, attended their celebrations, was invited to their family gatherings, welcomed in their homes, and sadly, attended their funerals as the years moved forward. I joined the North Coast Chapter of the Tuskegee Airmen (Cleveland) and was elected president a few years later—the first male, Caucasian president of a Tuskegee Airmen Chapter in the United States.

We routinely gave speeches at corporations, schools, civic clubs, and local military bases. I was getting to know the Tuskegee Airmen, their spirits, their worries, their joys, and the importance of their family harmony. The amazing standards that they held close to their hearts represented themselves as heroes of peace.

Only the Tuskegee Airmen offered me an opportunity to start my research because I had easy access to hundreds of them throughout the United States and had multiple opportunities to join their meetings, conventions, dedications, and reunions. I joined their national organization, participated with their activities, and learned their culture and values. This kind of opportunity to obtain such knowledge about the Airmen was not made available to me by any other hero or group of heroes. Without the Tuskegee Airmen's willingness to accept me into their culture as a friend, I would never have discovered the heroic values interwoven in their character; thus, I could never have written this book.

I taught my Tuskegee Airmen courses at Hiram College for many years. They became one of the most popular courses on campus. I ended many of these classes with a Tuskegee Airmen Banquet celebrating their accomplishments. Many Tuskegee Airmen and women attended these celebrations.

Teaching these values to my younger students created controversy
My first college class involving the Tuskegee Airmen was a class of adults—average age forty years. They loved the Tuskegee Airmen values and openly cried upon learning their sad history. Students were excited to start applying these special principles to their life. Being mature adults, they had experienced several of life's challenges. Many of them were married, some were divorced, others raised children, many changed jobs several times, and others suffered a major illness. They grew strong and matured from overcoming life's obstacles. They were middle aged people returning

to college to make a difference for themselves and their loved ones. Many had decided what kind of person they wanted to be and were taking steps to create that person. They were ambitious people filled with hopes for their future.

My second Tuskegee Airmen class consisted of eighteen-year-old freshmen. I was very eager to see my students' reaction to such positive and inspiring information. After several weeks of teaching the Tuskegee Airmen's history and values, my students asked me some very surprising questions:

"These values are wonderful, but how do they pertain to me?"

"How do you know these values will improve my life in my set of circumstances?

"Has anyone else used these values other than the Tuskegee Airmen?"

"Maybe these values only work for the Tuskegee Airmen in their particular situation."

"I am a teenage kid living in inner-city Cleveland; I am not in the military in 1941 being given the opportunity to fly airplanes."

"The Tuskegee Airmen had a rare opportunity in history—to become the first black aviators in the U.S. Military—and most of them were highly motivated individuals possessing college degrees before entering the service. They were at the right place and the right time in history. I do not think these values offer me a similar rare and unique opportunity."

Wow! What wonderful questions. I was really put on the spot by my insightful students. I was teaching heroic values for crisis-solving situations not knowing if these values worked equally well for anyone other than the Tuskegee Airmen. I started conducting similar research for other world heroes of peace to see if the fourteen heroic values are prevalent in their crisis decision making as well. I had much to do.

Two more years of research—famous heroes of peace compared to the Tuskegee Airmen

For the next two years, my students and I researched the problem-solving skills and values of famous humanitarian leaders. My students joined my research by completing hundreds of comparison-contrast essays describing how Nelson Mandela used similar values as the Tuskegee Airmen to reach comparable peaceful results amidst the political unrest in South Africa. Dr. Martin Luther King Jr. was shown to use the Airmen's values in many of his crisis situations in Montgomery, Alabama.

Other famous world heroes of peace

I continued my research in investigating famous world heroes of peace who are known for their understanding, compassion, and trust. I found that heroes dedicated to the betterment of mankind through their personal commitment and sacrifices did indeed utilize the fourteen values as they tried to improve the world. The fourteen values themselves—Courage, Trust, Judging, etc. —are certainly not new to anyone. Remember, the enlightening discovery of my research has been how my researched heroes of peace applied these values in a crisis, how they used these values to maintain the self-esteem of their enemies, and how they embraced these values to show compassion and trust while addressing prejudice and hate—my discovery is the applications of the values, not their definition.

By studying for years the biographies and accomplishments of famous heroes (Nelson Mandela, Desmond Tutu, Albert Schweitzer, Dr. Martin Luther King Jr., Mother Teressa, Abraham Lincoln), I was able to determine that most of their guiding values used for their problem-solving skills were the same values previously discussed. After all, these are well-known values associated with kind, respectful, and compassionate people.

When I wasn't traveling searching for heroes of peace, I continued teaching at Hiram College and researching heroes of peace. I also taught Hiram College students attending Cuyahoga Community College, Lorain County Community College, and Lakeland Community College. I continued researching other heroes of peace around the world, and I continued working with my students comparing the accomplishments and values of these magnificent people with the Tuskegee Airmen.

A system of values accessible to anyone, to benefit all people

My students were impressed when realizing many other world heroes of peace used the same values as a basis for their crises decisions as the Tuskegee Airmen. Some students had taken the approach that the Tuskegee Airmen's value system was too good to be true. When my students realized that my other selected heroes of peace also used the same problem-solving and conflict resolution techniques, the validity and strength of the Tuskegee Airmen value system was greatly reinforced.

Most of my students were very inspired by the Tuskegee Airmen's accomplishments and felt motivated and encouraged about the future success of their own lives if they could embody these values. Showing that other world heroes of peace also utilized the heroic values was very encouraging giving my students trust in the values. However, there was still a percentage of the less-confident students, who stated:

> "Many of my researched world leaders of peace had opportunities, assets, friends, and political connections that greatly helped them accomplish their seemingly impossible tasks. For example, although Nelson Mandela was poor as a child, his father was chief of their tribe and not without influence. I doubt similar opportunities will come into my life."

> "Professor Cram, I have seen no evidence that these values you discovered work for the uneducated and the poor."

> "Yea, if you're rich, famous, or have influential contacts these heroic values seem to have great merit. I have yet to see examples of how these heroic values empowered poor people living in a slum to accomplish great things."

Finding Heroes of peace among the impoverished with fewer assets than my students

Now my students sent me out into the world on a second challenge. My quest was to find heroes of peace who had fewer assets and opportunities than any of my students. I had to locate heroes living in poverty, or children perhaps, using similar heroic values to accomplish amazing deeds.

Are my discovered heroic values only found in highly educated and gifted individuals, or do they also exist in the average person as well, even among the illiterate and destitute? I tried to locate heroes among the impoverished for the next seven years. If I could succeed in this challenge, then my doubting students might realize, by employing my discovered heroic values into their lives, that multitudes of opportunities will be within their reach.

My new research took me twice to South Africa. I interviewed local heroes living in the Cape Town townships (slums) of Guguletu and Khayelitsha, in the Johannesburg township of Soweto, and Port Elizabeth's Area Q. Some of these townships had one water faucet for every 600 people and one doctor for every 30,000 individuals. The unemployment rate was often over 60% and the percentage of those carrying the HIV AIDS virus often exceeded 40%.

On four separate occasions, I traveled to Nicaragua, the second poorest country in the Western Hemisphere next only to Haiti. Nicaragua's population is 5.3 million with 4 million living on less than $1 per day. I interviewed families and children living off the city dump in Chinandega, visited families living in dilapidated shacks up in the northern mountains of Somoto, and participated in community tours and meetings in the remote fishing village of El Minco on the southern shore of Lake Nicaragua. I toured a hospital in Managua for pregnant women (two women occupied each cot) and interviewed many of the doctors and nurses.

One new-born child in this hospital was in a glass incubator with a plastic bag outside her body housing some of her intestines. I asked a doctor if the child was born that way. His reply was "No, she was born on the Managua City Dump in a pile of garbage. Her mother, walking through the dump looking for food, stopped long enough to squat and give birth to her. Afterwards, her mother kept walking abandoning the child in the refuse. The infant was then attacked by several wild dogs ripping open her abdomen and causing facial injury. A passer-by, also looking for food, grabbed the baby from the wild dogs, cut the umbilical cord to leave the afterbirth for the ravenous canines, and ran half a mile to the main highway. Covered in blood, she boldly stood in front of the first car and a screeching of brakes confirmed she was seen by the driver. Holding the infant's entrails in her hand, she had little trouble convincing the driver to take her to the hospital. As miraculous as it seems, the baby will be fine. Several nurses in the hospital expressed interest in adopting the infant.

When I speak of poverty in this book, I am not talking about people working part-time for minimum wage living in a housing project. By comparison, such individuals are rich.

Was I successful searching for heroes among the poor?

Over this seven-year period, was I successful in locating heroes with far fewer assets and opportunities than any of my students? Absolutely. Were any of these individuals highly successful, accomplishing difficult tasks, and helping hundreds of people using values similar to my selected world heroes of peace? Yes.

I stopped my search when I had found eighty heroes of peace from forty-three different countries. I believed eighty heroes was enough to substantiate my findings. Upon researching these eighty heroes, which included Benjamin O. Davis Jr. representing the Tuskegee Airmen, I found they all utilized compassionate applications of the fourteen Values of Peace —which was to be expected.

Key Point

I selected heroes who fit my criteria of solving problems peacefully. Many of my heroes are deceased while others are still in the prime of their lives. I intentionally searched for and discovered heroes of both genders, from a large cross section of cultures, religious beliefs, economic status, nationalities, ages, and educational levels. My selected heroes consist of 38-females, 42-males, 14-children, 11-statespersons, 3-scientists, 1 former child soldier, 3-born into slavery, 22-born into poverty, 13-Nobel Peace Prize winners, 19-went to jail for their cause, 80-dedicated and compassionate heroes of peace and human dignity serving those in need from forty-three different countries. Common, shared, and identical human goodness from people all over the world.

As you continue to read, you will meet the Flower Man, an individual living in a slum and supporting ten families with sixty children by picking up discarded beer cans from the street and turning them into works of art.

When a man is creative and ambitious enough to start a successful business from trash left in the streets, it is difficult for any of my students—or anyone else for that matter—to claim they do not have the wherewithal or connections to become successful or to make a positive difference in the world.

In addition to the Flower Man, you will meet several other heroes of peace also living among the impoverished. All have achieved success through helping thousands of individuals. All employ the values of my original world heroes of peace and routinely produce what many consider to be unbelievable accomplishments.

The Tuskegee Airmen became incredible warriors while employing peaceful means to overcome prejudice, injustice, and discrimination in the United States military. Nelson Mandela and Desmond Tutu found peaceful ways of providing heroic leadership to people during an extremely violent and suppressive regime—the Apartheid government of South Africa.

Ginetta Sagan, founder of Amnesty International in the United States, has peacefully liberated thousands of political prisoners and fought for human rights in Nazi Germany, Vietnam, Chile, Poland, South Africa, Czechoslovakia, and elsewhere. She is a tiny woman barely five feet tall who attracted the attention of every national leader in the world, especially the bad ones. She is famous for stating, "Silence in the face of injustice is complicity with the oppressor."

Booker T. Washington was born a slave. At the age of 26 he became principal of the Tuskegee Institute, a school he created in Alabama for blacks. Because of the high level of prejudice and bigotry at the time, there was little state funding to build the school. In fact, the State of Alabama offered Booker T. Washington so little money, that it was felt he could not succeed building his school and would surely quit. But he did not quit. He was not offered enough money to hire laborers, so his future students built the school as volunteers. He was not offered enough money to buy bricks, so he had his future students make bricks from the Alabama-clay soil. Then they built the school brick-by-brick in 1881. This original building still stands today (2021), as I can attest, having toured it in 2006.

Understand that several years had passed since my first class of freshman doubted that the Tuskegee Airmen values would work for them and my returning from South Africa finding impoverished heroes of peace using the same values. As I returned to Hiram College after my traveling research, I addressed a new class of students that had to be brought up to date on my research. For seven years, I researched the heroic values of peace among the impoverished and presented them to my poorer students at Hiram College. I can safely say that all my latest students understood that the Heroes' Values are beneficial for them to enrich their lives and accomplish great things.

Eighty Heroes of Peace

In the Appendix you will find a list of all eighty of my selected heroes of peace. I have indicated my selected hero's name, the county of their operations, and their area of aid to humanity. I strongly encourage you to read about some of these amazing individuals by doing additional research on your own. I use many of their reinforcing and inspiring quotes throughout this book.

True heroes of peace behave with dignity when they are being treated with disrespect. When verbally attacked, especially when witnessed by others, this ability shines like a mastery of confidence and control. This remarkable skill also intimidates their attacker often encouraging them to lighten their stance or look for a retreat with dignity. You will shortly see, these discovered heroes' values are invaluable offering the keys to peace, safety, dignity, and success. This book discusses 25 of the 80 world heroes of peace from my research:

1. Principal Daniels South Africa—principal of an elementary school where street gangs filled the school buildings with bullet holes and used the youth for prostitution.

2. Glenys van Halter Khayelitsha, South Africa—picked up endangered and abused children from slum streets and started teaching them schoolwork under a tree.

3. Reverend Corine McClintock Roodepoort, South Africa—rescued infants in garbage dumps dying from AIDS while building a complete village to care for them.

4. Ryan Hreljac Winnipeg, Canada—started at five years old, raising money for water wells in Africa.

5. Hannah Taylor Winnipeg, Canada—started at five years old raising money and finding homes and jobs for the homeless.

6. Hal Reichle Bedford, Ohio, the United States—a wonderfully mysterious and enchanting man, who spent his life secretly giving anonymously to total strangers.

7. Efren Penaflorida Philippines—at sixteen years old, started a portable classroom on a cart for slum children in the Philippines.

8. Nelson Mandela South Africa—fighting for equal rights and freedoms.

9. Olga Sanchez Mexico—rescuing migrants fleeing oppression who have lost arms and legs from falling under the train of death.

10. Gilbert Doho Cameroon, Africa—teaching women's rights by using street and community theater as a tool.

11. Masalakulangwa Mabula Malawi, Africa—a street child from age five to twelve years old, later returning to the streets with two master's Degrees and being an Anglican priest to rescue other street children.

12. Paul Harris Chicago, Illinois—an attorney who started a businessman's group and ended up changing the lives of millions and millions of people around the world.

13. Irena Sendler Germany—smuggled out hundreds of infant children from the Warsaw Ghetto saving them from the Nazi death camps.

14. Claw Lady Khayelitsha, South Africa—anonymous locator of destitute children whose parents have died from HIV/AIDS.

15. Father Marco Dessy and **16. Frank Huezo** Partners of Peace with Father Marco Dessy (above). Chinandega, Nicaragua—rescued thousands of children living on a garbage dump by providing food housing, and education.

17. John Robert Lewis United States—civil rights, equality, equal opportunity

18. Dr. Meena Patel India—defends women's rights for education, health, and employment while providing sanitation, employment, and health services

19. Booker T. Washington USA—Human rights, principal of the Tuskegee Institute

20. Benjamin O. Davis Jr. USA—Commander of the Tuskegee Airmen

21. Eleanor Roosevelt First Lady to President Roosevelt—advocate of equality

22. Ginetta Sagan Founder of Amnesty International in the United States

23. Abraham Lincoln Sixteenth president of the United States

24. Mother Teresa Caring for the wretched poor

25. The Flower Man Entrepreneur for the poor

The rarest of heroes: the hero of peace

What fascinated me was the comparison of these heroes to others who have often been called heroes: General George Custer, General George S. Patton, Napoleon Bonaparte, Josef Stalin, Alexander the Great, Vladimir Lenin, Senator Joseph McCarthy, and Karl Marx. These famous figures did not solve their problems peacefully, benefiting all concerned. When I compared the motivations and values they used to solve their problems, few, if any, of the fourteen values appeared.

Character is based on free-will choice. To understand someone's character, you must understand that person's value system. Our values define our character and guide our words and actions.[3]
Dr Paul A Wright, Youngstown, Ohio

Persistence would be required

Please understand, the greatest joy a human being can experience, the highest satisfaction and self-worth imaginable, and the opportunity to overwhelmingly justify why we are alive, is quietly waiting for us in the hands-on service to others. As I was writing this book I knew, if I ingrain into my character the magnificent leadership skills and problem-solving abilities of these remarkable heroes, should I not use these new skills for the benefit of myself and others? Why would I arm myself with these powerful heroic tools of peace if I were not going to use them? I told myself to concentrate on the value of persistence, for I had a long and obstacle-laden journey ahead of me.

The greatest glory in living lies not in never falling,
but in rising every time we fall.
Nelson Mandela

Darkness can't drive out darkness; only light can do that.
Hate can't drive out hate; only love can do that.
Martin Luther King Jr.

Don't let someone else create your world for you, for when you do,
it is always too small.
Ed Cole

---

3 Dr. Paul A. Wright, *Mother Teresa's Prescription, Finding Happiness and Peace in Service*, ave maria press, Notre Dame, Indiana 2006

II. The Tuskegee Airmen

A Brief History—Discovering their Heroic Values

We have the power to guide and encourage what is meant to be.
Carol Ruggie (Co-founder Modeling Future Heroes)

*Each one has to find his peace from within. And peace to be real must be
unaffected by outside circumstances.*
Mahatma Gandhi

Do what you feel in your heart to be right. You will be criticized anyway.
Eleanor Roosevelt

NOTE: Alabama Indians are the namesake for the State of Alabama, a territory they originally occupied. This land was occupied by the Tuskegee Indians prior to the Alabama tribe. I found little history about the Tuskegee Indians. Many historians, however, believe the word "Tuskegee" in the Alabama Indian's language meant "warrior."

I selected the fourteen values and their associated actions simply because they are the ones that came to my attention, the ones that my students and I observed most frequently during our research into the Airmen. You might ask me, "Are there not additional positive values other than these fourteen?" Of course, there are, but again, these are the ones that stood out in our study of the Airmen; therefore, these are the ones we researched. Most heroic values have synonyms. For example, my researched value of Compassion would probably be identical to kindness, benevolence, consideration, charity, and generosity. I could have selected any of those words to represent the studied value of Compassion.

You might ask as well, "Did all 14,000 of the Tuskegee Airmen always behave so magnificently?" Of course not. Everyone has bad days. Sometimes we behave well, other times poorly. My chosen fourteen values were determined from the Tuskegee Airmen that I studied, from documents and books that I researched, and from countless stories the Airmen told me throughout the years. I researched and studied about 100 Airmen. I learned that the Tuskegee Airmen's behavior, under adverse conditions, was consistently higher in caliber than was the behavior of many other human beings under similar circumstances. This will become very apparent as you keep reading. I also concentrated on the Airmen's behavior when they were at their best. This is where the high caliber of character existed that I came to understand. I researched "why" this was true. What follows are some true events supporting the Airmen's values.

This chapter describes the amazing, sad, and inspiring history of the Tuskegee Airmen. In these pages I present several situations where the Tuskegee Airmen's remarkable conduct during a crisis caught my attention. I want the reader to see the process I used to discover these values by studying the crisis-solving skills of these heroes of peace. At the end of this chapter, I list my finalized fourteen Heroic Values of Peace and the action used to apply them from my lengthy study of the Tuskegee Airmen's magnificent behavior. The heroic events presented in this chapter substantiate how the Tuskegee Airmen demonstrated the 14 values, and therefore the events are presented according to the values they exemplify rather than in chronological order.

My future research—what I needed to discover
To be sure, the Tuskegee Airmen did not have a written problem-solving methodology. They did not follow a thought-out plan to solve their problems. They did not have the list of their values that I discovered during my

research. They were not aware that most of them were using a similar set of values in making their critical decisions. There were about 14,000 Tuskegee Airmen stationed in the United States, Europe, and Northern Africa. They were all raised by different parents and attended different schools. How could most of their problem-solving values of peace be similar?

Am I suggesting that many of the Tuskegee Airmen leaders, regardless of where they were stationed in the world, regardless of the prejudicial problems they were facing, seemed to peacefully resolve their crises while employing the values that I researched? Yes, I am saying that. Am I also suggesting that many of the Airmen employed a similar problem-solving methodology to resolve their crises peacefully? Yes, I am saying that as well. How can that be? Now you know why I am so excited.

In Chapter one, I listed the fourteen heroic attributes or values my students and I discovered were used most often by the Tuskegee Airmen to succeed in peacefully resolving their conflicts. The rest of this chapter will give some of the remarkable behavior choices used by the Tuskegee Airmen allowing my students and me to discover these fourteen values.

CHOOSING THE VALUE OF BEHAVIOR. I often treated other people similarly to how they treated me. If someone was disrespectful to me, I was often disrespectful in return. The Tuskegee Airmen were routinely treated with disrespect, yet their return behavior was usually admirable. It was inspiring to see how the Tuskegee Airmen continually *behaved* with respect and dignity toward those degrading them. Here are some examples.

Could I do what the Tuskegee Airmen did?

How successful would I be if my employer told me to work on a complex and lengthy project, then failed to support my work, reduced my needed funding, prevented me from receiving the necessary tools, refused to furnish me the required support, would not repair my broken equipment, and then turned in false reports to management about my inefficiency and incompetence? Success under these circumstances would be very doubtful. However, the Tuskegee Airmen succeeded beyond all expectations under such conditions. How?

Blacks in the military had been researched and officially found to be incompetent to be in combat

The United States War Department, between 1924 and 1939, asked the Army War College in Montgomery, Alabama, to study the intelligence and ability of the black man for military combat positions should another war become a reality. The War College study, conducted by freshmen students at the institution, concluded that blacks lacked intelligence, had 25% smaller brains by weight than whites, were cowardly under combat conditions, were superstitious, and did not have the ability to operate complicated machinery like airplanes, tanks, and heavy artillery. The report also indicated that the capillaries in a black man's eyes were too small to withstand the pressures of pulling out of a dive in an aircraft.[4] The reports stated that opportunities for blacks in the military should increase to meet labor demands but stated they should always be segregated from whites, not be allowed to operate complex machinery, and never be placed in a position of command.

A dark sadness in our military history

This prejudicial War Department Report on the intelligence and ability of the black man for military combat was used as a measuring stick for their abilities for the next twenty years. This degrading report is partially responsible why blacks in the military were primarily utilized as road builders, janitors, and mess cooks. There were no black pilots or aircraft mechanics. In all the military, there were only four black officers, and three of them were chaplains.

Despite this horrible treatment, the majority of Tuskegee Airmen *behaved* with respect. The white military supervisors tried very hard to get the Airmen to respond with anger, revenge, and contempt. These white supervisors were not successful in this endeavor.

The Tuskegee Airmen and Women were the first black military pilots and support crews in the United States military. They started in March of 1941 at the beginning of World War II under the command of the U.S. Army Air Corps (the United States Air Force was not created until September 18, 1947). Although the publicity indicated the Tuskegee Airmen experience was an opportunity to establish the black man's capability in warfare, the program was secretly controlled by an undercurrent to prove, once and for all, that they were incapable of flying military aircraft in combat. The black-flying program was under the operational authority of southern raised and cultured military officers and politicians—and they were determined for this "foolish undertaking" to fail. It did not fail, however, for the Tuskegee Airmen set records back in the 1940s that still have not been matched today. How?

---

4 Video, *Flying for Freedom, Untold Stories of the Tuskegee Airmen*, AMS Production Group, 2007

THE VALUE OF CREATING CHANGE. Critics were trying to change the Tuskegee Airmen by using condemnation and prejudicial treatment. Yet the Tuskegee Airmen were trying to change their critics by performing with examples of excellence. I would love to learn how to react to negativity with such positive intents. The Tuskegee Airmen brought about positive change after experiencing negative and degrading hardships. What follows are examples I found where the Tuskegee Airmen repeated this outstanding methodology for creating positive *change*.

The only black man at West Point

In 1932, Benjamin O. Davis, Jr., a black male, was awarded entrance into West Point from the recommendation of Congressman Oscar S. DePriest, the only black congressman in the United States. Benjamin Davis Jr. was then the only black cadet in West Point and was put through the silent treatment all four years of the program. No one spoke to him other than for training. He had no roommate. He was kept segregated. Every Sunday meal, he had to ask permission to eat at eighty-five mess-hall tables. He was usually denied permission to eat at his first attempt and was forced to inquire at the next table, sometimes until all eighty-five tables had been approached. Davis addressed this insulting degradation with calmness and dignity. Every degrading action was done on purpose to encourage Davis to quit West Point and discourage him from graduating, for if he graduated from West Point he would be an officer, and no one would obey the orders given by a black officer. This unfair prejudicial treatment of Davis reinforced the need to show that blacks were as competent as whites. This discrimination showed how far they had to progress to be considered equal with whites. It revealed how high the level was of inequality emphasizing the huge gap needing to be closed. This reinforced Davis' goal, making him more resolved. In 1936, he graduated from West Point in the top 10% of his class and was now a real problem for the United States Army. What to do with a black officer? [5] He was shipped out to the 24th Infantry Labor Pool in Kansas where it was intended for him to assimilate, to be forgotten, and not to be a problem. You will discover as you continue reading, he would soon be charged with the success or failure of the Tuskegee Airmen pilot program.

---

5 *The Tuskegee Airmen, Victory at Home and Abroad*, Benjamin O. Davis Jr. by Sarah Specht, Central Alternative High School, 39 Bluff Street, Dubuque, IA 52001 started June 1997

I was silenced solely because cadets did not want black cadets at West Point.
Their only purpose was to freeze me out. What they did not realize was
that I was stubborn enough to put up with their treatment to reach
the goal I had come to attain.
Benjamin O. Davis Jr.

What a positive way for Davis to create change. Today, West Point has a plaque commemorating Benjamin O. Davis Jr., and a new barracks named after him. Davis endured four years of prison-type isolation at West Point. Davis stated, "Living as a prisoner in solitary confinement had not destroyed my personality, nor poisoned my attitude toward other people."[6]

What were some of the Tuskegee Airmen's motivations that kept them focused?

The Tuskegee Airmen had several goals for CHANGE that they wanted to accomplish.[7]

- To become the first black fighter and bomber pilots in the United States Army Air Corps
- To become the first black aircraft mechanics and flight crews in the United States Army Air Corps
- To prove that their abilities were equal to those of whites', and in doing so
  - » help integrate the Armed Services
  - » pave the way for equal jobs with whites in the military
  - » pave the way for civilian equal rights and employment opportunities for their future generations.
  - » pave the way for better educational opportunities in the military and at home
- Promote careers in aviation for American youth
- To make their families, friends, and others proud of their service and accomplishments
- To serve as examples of excellence, creating hope, self-esteem, and perseverance
- To serve as examples of excellence for whites encouraging confidence, equality, trust, and future employment opportunities

---

6 *Army Times,* by Kevin Lilley, "West Point barracks to honor Tuskegee Airmen leader." March 17, 2015
7 Told to the author by many Tuskegee Airmen during hundreds of personal interviews.

People often ask me if several of the Tuskegee Airmen's accomplishments were related to their fear of being disbanded. Of course they were, but we all need to carefully evaluate our priorities. As we have discussed, the Tuskegee Airmen were regularly subjected to demeaning and humiliating treatment. Also discussed was one of the reasons this disgraceful treatment existed. The prejudicial perpetrators wanted the Tuskegee Airmen to get angry, to strike back, and retaliate against the cruel treatment of their Army Air Corps supervisors. If the Airmen's retaliation occurred, the black flying experiment would be deemed a failure, the Tuskegee Airmen would be declared too unmanageable to be molded into disciplined pilots, and the program would be discontinued.

Benjamin O. Davis Jr. knew this very well. He kept a close watch on the behavior of his men, discouraging anything but responsible behavior and

Benjamin O. Davis Jr. the day he soloed.

positive responses to the cruel treatment received. This may answer the many questions about "why" the Tuskegee Airmen put up with so much abuse. One might wonder how they managed their dignity or maintained their self-esteem. Simply because if they rebelled, they might be disbanded losing the opportunity to become fighter and bomber pilots in the United States Army Air Corps, foregoing the chance to become aircraft mechanics and flight crews, and not being able to prove that their abilities were equal to those of whites.

THE VALUE OF DEVELOPING VISION. Many individuals lose sight of their dreams when their dreams are discouraged, their pathways to success are blocked, and when the people they need assistance from are not supportive. Despite all the blockades experienced by the Tuskegee Airmen, they never lost sight of their hopes and goals. I never realized that having a wonderful *vision* was enough to persist through what seems to be insurmountable obstacles. I see now how the Tuskegee Airmen coupled vision with *perseverance* to enable future success. Even so, I'm sure it was difficult for the Airmen to look toward a bright future while constantly being threatened with failure and disbandment, given little support, and isolated from other troops.

Many of the southern military leaders, congressmen, senators, and government officials did not support the Tuskegee Airmen undertaking and encouraged its defeat. The fact that President Roosevelt ordered the formation and training of the Tuskegee Airmen did not matter to them. They felt confident that they could make the program fail by showing the black man's incompetence to fly. They were highly prejudiced against blacks and had generations of such beliefs repeatedly ingrained in their heritage.

The Tuskegee training started out with a demerit system. If there was any dust under a Tuskegee Airman's bunks, or if a coin could not bounce off their bed sheets, then a demerit was issued. Three demerits would get an airman kicked out of the program. From the first class of cadets, 60% were kicked out under this prejudicial system and not allowed to graduate. The first graduating class consisted of only five pilots. Benjamin O. Davis Jr. was one of them. The second training class lost 73% of their airmen to the demerit system with only three graduating cadets.[8]

There were no military black flying schools

However, President Franklin D. Roosevelt in 1940, because of mounting pressure from the NAACP and Cleveland and Pittsburgh newspapers, directed the Army Air Corps to consider an all-black flying unit to see if blacks could be taught to fly. Because military aviation schools were filled in preparation for WWII, some civilian schools were employed to assist. One such school was in Tuskegee, Alabama, near the Tuskegee Institute, an all-black college built by Booker T. Washington.

Eleanor Roosevelt was a true advocate for an integrated military. She had *vision*.

The First Lady, Eleanor Roosevelt, a determined advocate of an integrated military, was in favor of the Tuskegee flying school getting underway. You are about to find out why Eleanor Roosevelt is one of my Heroes of Peace, for she succeeded in most of her endeavors using peaceful, non-confrontational means.

On March 29, 1941, Eleanor Roosevelt, a photographer, and the required Secret Service agents, went to Tuskegee, Alabama, at the request of Dr. Frederick Douglas Patterson, president of the Tuskegee

8 *Black Knights, The Story of the Tuskegee Airmen*, by Homan, Lynn and Reilly, Thomas, Pelican Publishing 2001, Gretna, Louisiana

Institute. President Patterson needed funding to complete the airfield at the Tuskegee Institute, thus qualifying the institution to conduct pilot training and filling the requirement that a suitable airport must be within "ten miles" of the training facility. To raise money for the airfield, Patterson invited the Julius Rosenwald Fund of Chicago to hold their board meeting at the Tuskegee Institute. Coincidentally, Eleanor Roosevelt was on the Julius Rosenwald Fund's board of directors (the plot thickens).

Eleanor Roosevelt and Alfred Anderson in a Piper Cub airplane

Eleanor Roosevelt arrived early, giving President Patterson an opportunity to give her a tour of the Tuskegee Institute. During the tour, the First Lady watched an aerobatic flight demonstration by the civilian flight school there. After the flight demonstration and several take offs and landings, Alfred Anderson taxied his Piper Cub up to the grass parking area. There, standing watching him, was Eleanor Roosevelt, the first lady of the United States.

She was introduced to Alfred "Chief" Anderson and his crew of black flight instructors. Eleanor Roosevelt said to Anderson, "Some say Negroes can't fly airplanes, but you seem to be flying around very well. I want to go for a ride in your airplane." This request of hers was strongly discouraged by the Secret Service, but she paid them little attention. While Eleanor Roosevelt was strapping herself in the Piper Cub, the Secret Service Agents were threatening to call the president to stop her! [9]

After the First Lady got into the airplane, she requested her photograph be taken with Alfred Anderson by the photographer she brought with her.[10] Anderson flew Eleanor Roosevelt around the area for over one hour. The

9 The Eleanor Roosevelt Papers Project, Teaching Eleanor Roosevelt Glossary, The Tuskegee Airmen,
https ://www2.gwu.edu/æerpapers/teachinger/glossary/tuskegee-airmen.cfm
10 Ibid

photograph taken of Eleanor Roosevelt in an airplane with a black pilot appeared in newspapers all over the United States. Anderson stated to reporters about flying Eleanor Roosevelt, "It was a wonderful experience and very instrumental in reducing the prejudice against black pilots.[11]

Did Eleanor Roosevelt plan this whole adventure? Were these events part of her *vision*?

Did President Patterson know Eleanor Roosevelt was on the Board of Directors of the Julius Rosenwald Fund? A black pilot flying the First Lady in an airplane—that should turn some heads and help put to rest the argument that black men are not capable of safely flying aircraft. If black pilots are safe enough to fly the First Lady, they certainly should be able to fly military aircraft as well.[12]

The Tuskegee Institute received government approval for the black flying school in January of 1941, but it was contingent upon completing the construction of a suitable airfield. The Tuskegee Institute lacked the funding to finish this requirement.[13]

Perhaps the national publicity of Eleanor Roosevelt in an airplane with a black pilot and an annual meeting of the Julius Rosenwald Fund at the Tuskegee Institute with Trustee Eleanor Roosevelt present indicated some clandestine planning.

After the meeting at the Tuskegee Institute, the Julius Rosenwald Fund granted the Tuskegee Institute a $175,000 loan to finish Molton Field, which became the Tuskegee Institute's CPTP (Civilian Pilot Training Program). The runway complex was built, and Eleanor Roosevelt became devoted to supporting the Tuskegee Institute. It pays to have influential friends.

Eleanor Roosevelt commented in her newsletter *My Day*, "Finally we went out to the aviation field, where a Civil Aeronautics unit for the teaching of colored pilots is in full swing. They have advanced training here, and some of the students went up and did acrobatic flying for us. These boys are good pilots. I had the fun of going up in one of the tiny training planes with the head instructor and seeing this interesting countryside from the air." [14]

---

11 *Black Knights, The Story of the Tuskegee Airmen*, by Homan, Lynn and Reilly, Thomas, Pelican Publishing
2001, Gretna, Louisiana
12 Ibid
13 *Owlcation, Eleanor Roosevelt's Flight into History with a Tuskegee Airman*, by Ronald E. Franklin, December 13, 2017
14 Ibid

Who was Alfred "Chief" Anderson?

Alfred Anderson was turned down for flying lessons by every flying school in the three-state area because he was black. Not giving up, he borrowed $2,500 from his family and friends and bought a Piper Cub airplane and gradually taught himself to fly. Don't try this at home. Alfred Anderson later became one of the most famous of the Tuskegee Airmen pilots and a flight instructor. This process not only took *persistence*, but great *vision* as well.

On March 19, 1941, the War Department established the first black flying squadron. It was named the 99th Pursuit Squadron. The training was to take place at Chanute Field in Illinois until the Tuskegee Molton Field facility was constructed. On March 22, 1941, the Chanute Field training was activated.[15] After the $175,000 loan from the Julian Rosenwald Fund, the first class of black cadets arrived at Tuskegee to start their flight training in July of 1941. I would say Eleanor Roosevelt's peaceful and non-confrontational method of problem solving was most effective.

THE VALUE OF OVERCOMING OBSTACLES. When many obstacles are placed in the path of one's goals, discouragement and a lack of ambition are often the result. Hundreds of unfair, cruel, and unnecessary obstacles were placed in the path of the Tuskegee Airmen's goals, yet each obstacle seemed to be taken as an opportunity giving them more determination and strength.

I greatly admired how the Tuskegee Airmen viewed obstacles as opportunities for learning instead of impediments to their goals. Viewing obstacles as opportunities is a rare quality.

The Tuskegee flying school was secretly programmed for failure

Because of President Roosevelt's order, the U. S. Army Air Corps reluctantly started training black pilots at Tuskegee, Alabama. It would be advantageous to have a black officer help supervise these cadets. The only two black officers were Benjamin Davis Sr., and his son, Benjamin O Davis Jr., a recent graduate of West Point, and currently working at the 24th Infantry Labor Pool. Therefore, as a measure of expediency, Benjamin O. Davis Jr. was called from the 24th Labor Pool and enrolled in the first class of cadets at Tuskegee, Alabama. He was responsible for the success of the cadets. He could not have been more delighted.

---

15 *Red-Tailed Angels, The Story of the Tuskegee Airmen of World War 11*, Patricia and Fredrick McKissack, Walker and Company, NY 1995 pages 47-48

Benjamin O. Davis Jr. was sent to the assigned flight surgeon to take the necessary physical to qualify for pilot training. Davis flunked his physical exam because all black men flunked their physical exams. This was unwritten policy. Trumped up reasons like flat feet, bad teeth, or dizziness were fabricated. The flight surgeon who administered Davis' physical exam was not told that this man must pass the flight physical. Another flight surgeon was contacted, informed that the U.S. Army Air Corps wanted Davis to pass his flight physical; therefore, this second time he passed.[16]

To further emphasize the black man's inability to fly, most selected Tuskegee candidates were college graduates, many with advanced degrees, while the white fighter pilots were only required to have completed high school. Why? Perhaps to show that the best educated blacks would fail as fighter pilots when compared to less educated whites. This would hopefully send a powerful message to the world concerning the black man's ineptness. In other words, the project's intention was to fail, and the black pilots and their support crews knew this from the beginning. These obstacles had to be overcome peacefully.

Whenever I use the term Tuskegee Airmen, this also includes the Tuskegee Women. There were over 14,000 Tuskegee Airmen, which included women, with up to twelve Airmen needed to support each aircraft. All the pilots, mechanics, gunners, doctors, nurses, secretaries, parachute packers, control tower personnel, and support staff had to be black with few exceptions.

SUSTAINING THE VALUE OF SELF-ESTEEM. Few people who believe they are incapable are successful. Most people get their *self-esteem* from the approval and praises of others. The Tuskegee Airmen were fed a regular diet of criticism, admonishment, and degrading innuendo, yet their self-esteem remained high. How?

I was amazed how the Tuskegee Airmen maintained their high self-esteem while others continuously degraded, insulted, and treated them as third-class citizens. During my research, I located hundreds of other instances where the Tuskegee Airmen applied this same trait. Most people usually react harshly when they are degraded. Being able to react positively to demeaning treatment is one of the most powerful tools of peace there is, but it is also one the most difficult to learn.

---

16 Told to the author by Edith Roberts, Tuskegee pilot and wife of George Spencer Roberts, the first cadet in the Tuskegee Airmen Program. 2009

A plot to prove the Tuskegee Airmen were incompetent

The war was almost over in Northern Africa, so the Tuskegee pilots, with outdated aircraft and parts, had little chance to evolve as war heroes in that location. There were no German fighter planes to attack, but only a few left-over ground vehicles and trains. For months, the Tuskegee Airmen were restricted to missions involving only ground targets, like German trucks on some small Mediterranean islands. When several months had passed, reports were sent to Washington D.C. stating that none of the Tuskegee Airmen had shot down any German aircraft. This was part of the plan to show the Tuskegee Airmen were incapable of successfully flying military aircraft, especially in combat.

It was the government's intention to keep the Tuskegee pilots away from the enemy. It would be embarrassing for the southern political and military officials who were so vocal about the black man's inability to fly if the Tuskegee Airmen started shooting down enemy planes. The Tuskegee Airmen were also segregated and kept a secret from other military bases.

Other forms of harassment and prejudice were prolific

Donald Williams was a black draftsman assigned to the Tuskegee Airmen. His job was to prepare charts and graphs depicting the progress of the Tuskegee Airmen's flying program. Williams was the only black man employed in the white segregated portion of the base.

A few hours in the morning after starting work, his drafting tools (T-square, triangle, ruler) would need washing because of their regular contact with the graphite-pencil drawings. Williams was not allowed to use the "white only" washroom in his office to clean his drafting tools. Just outside his office, Williams waited six minutes for a bus which took him on a ten-minute bus ride to the segregated section of the base. There Williams used the bathroom facilities, washed his drafting tools as well, and waited another six minutes for the ten-minute bus ride back to his office. After working for another thirty minutes, it was time for lunch. Williams was not allowed to eat in the white section of the base, so he again waited six minutes for another ten-minute bus ride taking him to the segregated section of the base where he could eat. Complaints were filed against Williams because he was not getting enough work completed at his drafting desk. His self-esteem was maintained from knowing the quality of his work, from his ability to remain calm under extreme prejudice, and from his part in helping the war effort. Being the only Tuskegee cadet allowed to work in the white section of the base was ego-boosting as well.

Example is not the main thing in influencing others, it is the only thing.
Albert Schweitzer

The lack of media reporting on Tuskegee Airmen

The government frequently sent news correspondents to the white fighter bases, but never to the secret Tuskegee base. Any news coverage on the Tuskegee Airmen had to come from black reporters working for black newspapers and paying their own transportation overseas.

The Tuskegee Airmen shot down seventeen enemy aircraft in three days off the coast of Anzio, Italy, from January 27 to January 30, 1944. Not one white newspaper in the United States reported this amazing accomplishment. It was only covered in the Stars and Stripes. No one from any white press came to interview any Tuskegee Airmen.[17] Was this part of the plot to keep the Tuskegee Airmen a secret, encouraging their failure? They maintained their self-esteem from knowing what they have done, what they were capable of doing, not from others knowing as well.

How the Red Tails came to be

All the white fighter squadrons had their own insignia or markings on their fighters. For example, the 308th-fighter squadron had red, diagonal candy-stripes on their aircraft tails, the second fighter squadron had a yellow band just before the tail, and the 376th-fighter squadron had their tails painted as a yellow-and-black checkerboard. These insignias gave each squadron a sense of pride and recognition when entering combat, but the Tuskegee Airmen were kept a secret. They had no insignia markings.

Around June of 1944, as the P-51 Mustangs were being issued to the Tuskegee Airmen, a surplus of bright red "insignia" paint was discovered in a warehouse in Foggia, Italy. Being the only paint available, the mechanics decided to paint the empennage (tail section) and nose of their P-51s bright red. No other squadron had this insignia. Soon, as these red-tailed Mustangs were seen protecting and rescuing others, they became known as the Red Tails. The bomber pilots eventually called them the "red-tailed angels." The Red Tails soon became a symbol of Tuskegee Airmen's excel-

---

17 *The Black Knights, The Story of the Tuskegee Airmen* Lynn Homan and Thomas Reilly, Pelican Publishing Company, Gretna 2001

lence in performing their duties. Flying a red-tailed fighter plane was a great *self-esteem* booster. The German fighter pilots, who had learned the red-tail pilots were black, called them the "black birdmen." The Tuskegee Airmen, because they were completely segregated from other military units, called themselves the "Lonely Eagles."

Our government, encouraging the Tuskegee Airmen's failure, made six serious mistakes.

1. Prejudice against blacks in Southern United States was not just an attitude, it was a firm belief—ingrained in their culture. The southern-raised military commanders and politicians genuinely believed that blacks were incompetent and could never successfully fly fighter planes in combat. To prove this point, they wanted to show that college-educated blacks could not compete with high school-educated whites. Therefore, as previously mentioned, black Army Air Corps recruits initially had to have college degrees; white recruits were only required to have high-school educations.

2. Many of the Tuskegee recruits were removed from training through the prejudicial demerit system previously discussed. The treatment of the recruits was not supposed to be fair. It was designed to make them angry and encourage them to either rebel or quit. Because termination from the flying program resulted from the slightest mistakes, any recruit with the "right-stuff" to stay in the program, had to be exceptional. Therefore, the demerit system designed to terminate the program, inadvertently served to reduce the recruits to the finest of the finest.

3. A black officer was needed to oversee the Tuskegee recruits, and Benjamin O. Davis Jr. was selected. Few officers could match his ability, discipline, and excellent character as a commander. Benjamin Davis Jr. was one of the finest commanders anywhere that could have been put in charge of the program. He was chosen, however, because there were no other qualified black officers.

4. The initial commander of the Tuskegee training base was Colonial Frederick von Kimble and his right-hand hatchet man named Lt. Col. John T. Hazard (appropriately named). Kimble and Hazard hated blacks. They segregated drinking fountains and toilets, forbade social interaction with whites, and made it abundantly clear that no blacks would ever be promoted. On December 26, 1942, the day after Christmas, Noel Parrish was assigned as Tuskegee base commander replacing von Kimble. This was

an unintended Christmas present to the Airmen, for one of the first things Parrish did was remove the "white" and "colored" signs throughout the base. [18] He was not interested in crushing the self-esteem of the black pilots, but instead desired their success. In fact, Noel Parrish ate all his meals with the Airmen.

Parrish, aware of the lack of recreational activities for the Tuskegee recruits, encouraged black celebrities, like Lena Horne, Ella Fitzgerald, and Louis Armstrong to visit the base and entertain the Airmen.[19] Parrish proved that blacks could perform very well in leadership roles and flying competence in complete contradiction to the opinion of southern leaders.[20] Selecting Noel Parrish to command the Tuskegee Flying School was most instrumental in the program's success.

5. After their initial flight training at Tuskegee was completed, all the airmen were given their "wings" and became officers in the United States Army Air Corps. They were assigned to join white fighter squadrons in Europe, but no squadrons would accept them. "We don't want black pilots off our wings in combat!" The Tuskegee Airmen pilots and their support crews, not able to be deployed to join the war, remained in Alabama and went through their training again with the new recruits. Upon completion of their second training, they were assigned again to join an all-white fighter squadron in Europe, but again, the white squadron did not want them off their wing, so the Tuskegee pilots and their support crews remained in Alabama and went through their training a third time. I do not think training the Tuskegee Airmen cadets three times did anything other than make them super qualified. Big mistake!

Upon completion of their third training, again, no military units fighting the war overseas would accept them, so the Tuskegee pilots and their support crews—to justify the tax payer's expense for establishing their squadron—were sent to a completely isolated and fully segregated base in Morocco, Northern Africa, consisting of a dirt runway and tents for barracks. For all practical purposes, the war was over in this area. There were no German fighter planes at that location. This would assure the Tuskegee Airmen would not shoot down any enemy aircraft. This would help assure they could not prove themselves in combat. They had been set up again.

18 *Red-Tailed Angels, The Story of the Tuskegee Airmen of World War II,* Patricia and Fredrick McKissack, Walker and Company, NY 1995 page 67
19 *The Berkeley Daily Planet,* February 17, 2012, by Gar Smith, *The* Real *Story* of *the Tuskegee Airmen*
20 *Black Americans in Defense of Our Nation,* June 7, 2011, Sam Houston State University

6. Assigning the Airmen to shoot at ground targets like German trucks was an effort to keep them busy and out of the way. This action may have kept the Tuskegee Airmen from accumulating a record of enemy fighter plane kills; however, the repeated practice at attacking such small targets made the Airmen formidable and highly skilled opponents from the air.

I just listed six serious (unwise) mistakes our military and political officials made trying to discredit the Tuskegee Airmen. Each of these occurrences were intended to impede the Airmen's success, expected to make them appear incompetent, and designed to lower their self-esteem. But instead these challenges finely honed the Airmen's skills and developed them into one of the most formidable and well-disciplined forces ever known. Their self-esteem was maintained by their knowledge of their excellence. They knew who they were.

THE VALUE OF DISPLAYING COMPASSION. I find it difficult to treat with *compassion* those who mistreat me, to view with understanding and tolerance those who discredit and admonish me, yet the Tuskegee Airmen were compassionate to their most prejudicial critics and endeavored to serve with excellence those believing them incompetent. How?

The Tuskegee Airmen were able to demonstrate compassion toward those abusing them. This most unusual quality was repeated in all their endeavors.

Escorting bombers

American bombers were suffering heavy losses from German fighters; in fact, one mission consisting of 200 bombers, lost sixty-five bombers to German fighter planes and ground fire. The bomber escorts were Caucasian P-51 mustang pilots, and although they were very well trained and extremely talented pilots, they lived by the Army Air Corps' tradition, "I can chase an enemy fighter back to its homeland until I shoot it down." If our white P-51 fighter escort pilots pursued German fighters for miles until they successfully shot them down, who was guarding the bombers during their pursuit? This tradition left the bombers unprotected and Hitler knew it. The first wave of German fighters attacking our bomber formations fled the area as soon as they were attacked by the P-51 fighter escorts in hopes they would be pursued away from the bombers. As soon as our bombers were unprotected, a second wave of German fighters, waiting a few miles away, came in for the kill resulting in heavy bomber losses.[21]

---

21 Ibid

Eventually the Tuskegee Airmen were asked to escort our bombers. Benjamin O. Davis Jr. made it abundantly clear to each Tuskegee Airmen pilot, "If any German fighter shoots down a B-17 or B-24 bomber, the red-tailed pilot protecting the bomber had best be shot down first! Also, if any Tuskegee P-51 pilot left the bomber formation unprotected by pursuing a German fighter plane, he would be court marshaled and grounded for the rest of the war." [22][23]

To help successfully escort our bombers, the Tuskegee Airmen were given brand new P-51 Mustang fighter planes. Why? Because now they were protecting white bomber crews.

Although the existence of the Tuskegee Airmen was, for the most part, kept a secret, some bomber pilots had heard of the all-black fighter squadron. They initially expressed outrage that the lives of white bomber crews would be placed in jeopardy by assigning black pilots to escort them. But this feeling changed as the Tuskegee Airmen proved themselves. In fact, it was not long before white bomber crews were requesting the Tuskegee Airmen to escort their bombers. Did the whites like the Tuskegee Airmen? No. Did they trust them to keep them safe in combat? Yes.

There was not one Tuskegee Airmen Ace

If a fighter pilot were to shoot down five enemy planes, he would earn the coveted title of ace. This was a dream of most fighter pilots, to return home after the war as an ace. If the Tuskegee Airmen were such precision fighter pilots, how come none of them became an ace? The primary reason was the Tuskegee Airmen were there to protect the bomber crews, not build personal glory for themselves. When German fighters fled the American bombers expecting the Tuskegee Airmen fighters to give pursuit, they were surprised to find the Tuskegee Airmen stayed with the bombers. The red-tailed pilots showed such COMPASSION for the bomber crews, that they repeatedly sacrificed their chance of becoming an ace.

Bombers shot down by German fighters escorted by the Tuskegee Airmen

How many American bombers were shot down by German fighter planes while under Tuskegee Airmen escort? This number does not include any bombers shot down by ground guns. Multiple publications and sources say not one bomber was ever lost to enemy fighters. That would be 0% lost. This

---

22 *Military.com*, The Tuskegee Airmen, David Grayson, https://www.military.com/history/the-tuskegee-airmen.html, copyrighted 2018
23 *Red-Tailed Angels, The Story of the Tuskegee Airmen of World War II*, Patricia and Fredrick McKissack, Walker and Company, NY 1995

is a popular belief adding to the Tuskegee Airmen's mystique, but it is not true. In truth, German fighter planes shot down only seven bombers out of 2,871 bombers escorted by the Tuskegee Airmen during thirty-three missions. That means that on all bomber escort missions encountering German fighters, twenty-four one hundredths of one percent of the bombers were lost to German fighters. That is amazing! What a wonderful way to display compassion for the bomber crews. For evidence of this, see the appendix.

Many of the white bomber pilots had no idea their red-tailed escorts were black; they just knew they were the best. The red-tail insignia was not registered by the Army Air Corps as an official squadron marking; therefore, when a red-tailed fighter was spotted, no record could be found of who they were or what base they came from. The Red Tails were a mystery.

THE VALUE OF ADDRESSING COURAGE. One cannot be courageous unless one is afraid. Courage is behaving magnificently while experiencing fear. Whether fighting enemy aircraft or unfair reprisals from the U.S. Army Air Corps, the Tuskegee Airmen just kept facing fears with rational and compassionate reactions. The Tuskegee Airmen gathered their remarkable courage to continue operating in such risky conditions.

A remarkable air battle

On March 31, 1945, several Red Tails were assigned to strike multiple ground targets near Linz, Austria. During their strafing runs, they were discovered and attacked by seventeen German fighter planes consisting of Messerschmitt 262s (German fighter jets) and Focke-Wulf 190s. Out of the seventeen German fighters, the Tuskegee Airmen shot down thirteen. None of the P-51 Red Tails were destroyed. Enough said. Point made. [24]

Can an aircraft's machine gun disable a destroyer escort?

On June 25, 1944, Tuskegee Airmen pilots flying P-47 Thunderbolts and returning from a low-level attack mission, spotted a German destroyer escort in the Adriatic Sea at Trieste Harbor in Yugoslavia. The ceiling was low, about 500 feet above the ground. The Airmen had no bombs, only machine guns, and destroyer escorts are usually not destroyed from machine guns alone. As the Tuskegee Airmen flew over the Nazi ship, it opened fire. Two of the Tuskegee Airmen, Gwynne Peirson and Wendell Pruitt, turned and attacked the destroyer escort with their machine guns firing. What kind of courage is required to attack a German destroyer with a machine gun? It

---

24 *Red-Tailed Angels, The Story of the Tuskegee Airmen of World War* II, Patricia and Fredrick McKissack, Walker and Company, NY 1995 page 116

sounds like the story of David and Goliath. However, after the Airmen's attack on the ship, it started to smoke and then blew up.[25] How this could have happened has been debated for years. Some believe a mine could have been on deck and struck by the Airmen's bullets. Another theory is that the bombardment of machine gun fire from P-47s eventually penetrated the deck striking the destroyer's powder magazine, an area where all the ammunition was stored. This area was exceedingly small from the air, about the size of a small truck on a Mediterranean island. I can see where all that practice shooting at trucks has paid off. Need I say more? [26] In any case, they successfully immobilized[27] the German destroyer escort with only their machine guns. Gwynne Peirson successfully recorded the fate of the destroyer with his P-47 wing camera. This was a fortunate thing, because no one on the Tuskegee Airmen base would believe the incident until shown Peirson's developed film.[28]

The Tuskegee Airmen, as planned, had their critics

In August of 1943, Benjamin O. Davis Jr. was transferred from Italy (Sicily) back to the United States to form the new 332nd Fighter Group in Selfridge, Michigan. The 332nd Fighter Group combined the Tuskegee Airmen's 99th, 100th, 301st, and 302nd Fighter Squadrons into one fighting unit. Taking Davis's command in Sicily was Col. Momyer, a man of limited integrity who did not share Davis's exceptional opinion of the black Airmen. At this time, the Tuskegee Airmen had only shot down one enemy aircraft (there were almost no enemy aircraft in the area), Col. Momyer submitted the following unsatisfactorily report to the War Department shortly after Davis left for Selfridge, Michigan:

> Based on the performance of the 99th fighter squadron to date, it is my opinion that they are not of the fighting character of any squadron in this group. They have failed to display the aggressiveness and daring for combat that are necessary to be a first-class fighting organization. It may be expected that we will get less work and less operational time out of the 99th Fighter Squadron than any other squadron in this group.
>
> —Col. William Momyer

25 Ibid page 94

26 *The Tuskegee Airmen, The First Top Guns*, "The Last Hurrah" (Program) 2004 page 10

27 The destroyer was immobilized and taken out of service; it did not sink. The ship was the former Italian Destroyer Giuseppi Missori, a TA-22, and converted by Germany into a torpedo boat. *Eleven Myths about the Tuskegee Airmen* by Daniel Haulman New South Books, Montgomery, Alabama 2012

28 *Black Knights, The Story of the Tuskegee Airmen*, by Homan, Lynn and Reilly, Thomas, Pelican Publishing Company, 2001, Gretna, Louisiana

This report coupled with the typical rumor mill, resulted in *TIME* magazine printing an article on September 20, 1943, that the 99th Fighter Squadron might be disbanded and transferred to the Coastal Air Command. Further rumors and misunderstandings resulted in the *New York Daily News*, in their September 30, 1943, issue, claiming that the Tuskegee Airmen's 99th Fighter Squadron had been broken up and returned to the United States.

These false reports greatly concerned Benjamin O. Davis Jr. as well as the War Department. The authorities temporarily stopped the formation of the 332nd Fighter Group until the negative reports and rumors could be investigated. A committee was formed in Washington D.C., called the Advisory Committee on Negro Troop Policies, to investigate these questionable and damaging rumors. Benjamin O. Davis Jr. was requested to testify before the committee. He was ordered to travel from Michigan to Washington D.C. to substantiate or deny the credibility of the 99th Tuskegee Airmen. This was serious stuff. [29] [30] Were the Tuskegee Airmen going to be finally disbanded? Had those bigoted southern-military officials and politicians won at last?

Benjamin O. Davis Jr. was calm and professional as he testified before the Committee about the skills of the 99th Fighter Squadron's pilots. He explained quite easily that the 99th Fighter Squadron could not shoot down enemy aircraft that were not there. Almost all the Tuskegee Airmen's missions in Sicily were air-to-ground targets that were carried out with excellent precision. Davis further explained that the 99th Fighter Squadron was under the command of the 33rd Fighter Squadron supervised by Col. William Momyer, a man who was "obviously uninformed and patently unfair" in evaluating the 99th's performance. Furthermore, Col. William Momyer and his staff have "offered the 99th no cooperation in any operational matters."[31]

Benjamin O. Davis Jr. explained the high competency of his men in the 99th Fighter Squadron so well, so calmly, with such dignity and conviction, that the War Department decided to continue with the creation of the Tuskegee Airmen's 332nd Fighter Group with Benjamin O. Davis Jr. as its commander.

---

29 Ibid
30 *A-Train, Memoirs of a Tuskegee Airman* by Lt. Co. Charles W. Dryden, pages 141-142, Tuscaloosa, Alabama, the University of Alabama Press 1997
31 *The Tuskegee Airmen, Victory at Home and Abroad*, Benjamin O. Davis Jr. by Sara Schmerbach, Central Alternative High School, 39 Bluff Street, Dubuque, IA 52001 started June 1997 page 190

Efforts to prove the Tuskegee Airmen incompetent were repeatedly unsuccessful

Some of the Tuskegee Airmen were given worn-out and shot-up P-40 fighter aircraft that were not safe to fly. The intent was to show that black men could not fly aircraft, just another example of how prejudice and discrimination were used to make the Tuskegee training program a failure. A future report to Washington D.C. stating "We gave the black Tuskegee Airmen fighter planes, but apparently they were not able to fly them," was the intent. But the Tuskegee Airmen simply took all those worn-out aircraft apart and sorted their pieces into different piles. Then, for every five worn-out and shot-up aircraft they were given, the Tuskegee Airmen were able to create one good aircraft safe to fly—and fly them they did.

In 2010, I was giving a speech about the Tuskegee Airmen at Travis Air Force Base in California. My speech included the information about receiving worn-out and shot-up aircraft. After my speech, three original Tuskegee Airmen mechanics took me aside to add to my knowledge. They told me that the Tuskegee Airmen were often assigned to stand in formation along a parade route at white fighter bases. The formation line was in front of many fighter planes parked along the parade route. One out of every six Tuskegee Airmen fell back out of line while the remaining Airmen closed ranks. What did these Tuskegee Airmen do behind the line of Airmen standing at attention? They had tools with them and removed from the fighter aircraft in the flight line many of the parts they needed to repair the fighters at their base. They told me it was difficult to get replacement parts, being just another effort to help insure the Tuskegee Airmen's failure. They took the parts off airplanes owned by the Army Air Corp to repair fighter planes owned by the Army Air Corps. [32] Is that stealing?

THE VALUE OF PERSEVERANCE. Determination is necessary to continue one's quest despite encountered difficulties. It is rare when one has the *perseverance* to face adversity when success is not within reach. Yet the Tuskegee Airmen's perseverance rarely weakened even though it was evident they would not be successful in many of their goals. Perseverance helps determine the validity of their mission, not whether the mission will be successful. The Tuskegee Airmen had incredible perseverance. They were driven. It seems to me that they considered failures as steppingstones to a goal. I

---

32 Told to the author by several Tuskegee Airmen while I visited Travis Air Force Base in California on November 8, 2004.

researched many other instances where the Tuskegee Airmen repeated this outstanding characteristic.

You can fight to save our lives, but you cannot swim with us

Tuskegee Airmen pilot Hiram E. Mann was flying his fighter plane off the coast of Anzio, Italy, during the battle of Anzio which took place from January 22, 1944, through June 5, 1944. During this campaign, many Tuskegee Airmen aided allied troops by shooting down German fighters, destroying ground targets, and supporting allied forces on the ground. Hiram Mann was instrumental in securing a beachhead by supporting from the air our allied ground troops.

Hiram Mann went to visit the beachhead by ground transportation a few days later. He noticed many of the soldiers he helped to secure the beach were enjoying themselves swimming in the Tyrrhenian Sea. Hiram Mann attempted to join their festivities and share in the accomplishment of securing the area from the enemy, but because Mann was black, he was not allowed to swim with the whites in the sea. He was told to leave the area. Mentioning that he helped defend and support these troops from the air a few days earlier had little bearing on his acceptance to go swimming. The troops whose lives he had saved asked him to leave [33] I cannot imagine the emptiness and frustration Hiram Mann felt at that moment. But he was determined to persevere and continue protecting those who hated him. He would not quit.

What did we fight for?

While I was teaching my Tuskegee Airmen classes at Hiram College, I sent students into Cleveland and Akron to interview several original Tuskegee Airmen. The questions I needed answered were, "Why did you want to fight for a country that did not want you, that did not respect you, that treated you with prejudice?" What was the motivation behind your perseverance to fight and die (75 Tuskegee Airmen lost their lives)[34] for a country who treated the enemy (Nazi soldiers) with more respect and dignity than you? What did the Tuskegee Airmen see in this country that allowed them to fight for its freedom amidst the many laws of hate and segregation against blacks?

---

33 Information derived from a one-hour personal interview between the author and Hiram E. Mann in 2007.
34 Told the author by William Holton, National Tuskegee Historian, in a personal interview, August 2004, National Tuskegee Airmen Convention, Omaha, Nebraska. National Tuskegee records claim 66 deaths.

When my students and I asked Arthur Sanders[35] these questions, he acted confused and surprised—almost offended. "What other country could we fight for?" Saunders inquired, "Despite how poorly we are treated, this is the only country we have." Saunders continued, "We are fighting to defeat Nazi Germany and to defeat the hate and prejudice against blacks, not only in the Army Air Corps, but in the United States. We have to improve the future for our children! If we quit, we have lost."

The Tuskegee Airmen courageously fought for the United States under continued prejudicial treatment. They shot down or disabled 260 German aircraft and were awarded eight Purple Hearts, ninety-five Distinguished Flying Crosses, and 744 Air Medal Clusters.

Returning to the United States

Upon their return to United States after the war, the Tuskegee Airmen left the transport ship's gangplank and were escorted away from the returning white military. They were told by military personnel at the bottom of the gangplank, "Whites to the right; blacks to the left!"[36] The white military went on to a hero's welcome involving celebrations, press coverage, and main-street ticker-tape parades. The Tuskegee Airmen were put on a bus or train and sent home. They returned to Jim Crow laws,[37] segregation, white-only drinking fountains, and back-of-the-bus second-class citizenry. Many of the drinking fountains labeled "colored only" had no plumbing connected to them. Very few people in the United States had ever heard of the Tuskegee Airmen, let alone what they had accomplished. The Tuskegee Airmen had returned to the same country they had left, one of hate, discrimination, and prejudice. Nothing had changed despite all their courageous victories![38]

Three Tuskegee Airmen officers in uniform, while being sent home on a train from New York, were asked to give up their seats, not for white officers, but for captured German prisoners. One of these three officers, Harold Brown, PhD, remembers the incident with a heavy heart.[39]

Tuskegee Airmen Dabney Montgomery was in the dining car of a train taking him home. He was asked to pull the shades on a train window while traveling in the dining car after dark. The Pullman porter requesting

---

35 Lieutenant Arthur Saunders, 477th Medium Bombardment Group, Tuskegee Airmen, living in Cleveland
36 Video, *Flying for Freedom, Untold Stories of the Tuskegee Airmen*, AMS Production Group, 2007
37 Jim Crow laws were state and local statutes that legalized racial segregation and denied equal rights to blacks.
38 Video, *Flying for Freedom, Untold Stories of the Tuskegee Airmen*, AMS Production Group, 2007
39 *The Berkeley Daily Planet*, February 17, 2012, by Gar Smith, *The Real Story of the Tuskegee Airmen*

this action stated that whites would often shoot at blacks in passing trains if seen traveling in a white-only dining car.[40]

Many black soldiers, in uniform, were welcomed home with violence. Reports of black soldier lynching's were not uncommon. One black soldier attempted to use the white restroom facilities at a bus stop. He was beaten so badly that he lost sight in both his eyes. Another black soldier name Hosea Williams took a drink from a white-only drinking fountain in Atlanta, Georgia. He was assaulted so severely he was left for dead by his assailants. They stopped the assault when they could no longer feel a pulse.

Hosea Williams did survive. He stated in an interview about his service in the military during the war, "I came home from the war, and nothing had changed. What did I fight for? Why did I even go over there? Was I even on the right side?" Williams continued to comment about the black military's uncommon perseverance, and how it did produce favorable outcomes for both the military and civilian citizens.

In 1972, Lt. Col Alexander Jefferson, a Tuskegee Airman and P-51 pilot and an endorser of this book, called a meeting of other airmen to his home in Detroit. This was the start of a national Tuskegee Airmen organization with more than 50 separate clubs. They all promoted their history by giving thousands of speeches at schools, civic groups, and corporations continuously pursuing equal rights for over fifty years. Two movies have been made, several documentaries, and many books were written as they persistently pursue their message.

It is now the year 2021. Brig. General Charles McGee and Lt. Col. Alexander Jefferson are both over 100 years old—still promoting the Tuskegee Airmen legacy. Most of the Tuskegee Airmen are deceased. It is not the end of an era; however, for many military historians, relatives, and friends of the Tuskegee Airmen, like me, are still promoting their amazing abilities. *Perseverance* must never stop; if it does, it's not perseverance.

THE VALUE OF ENCOURAGING TRUST. People who are thought to be inferior and unreliable are usually not trusted. Yet military personnel believing the Tuskegee Airmen to be incompetent, developed an unshakable trust in their abilities. The Tuskegee Airmen were able to earn and maintain *trust* from others, especially from those who disliked them—to earn the trust of their adversaries.

---

40 *Nightfighters, The True Story of the 332 Fighter Group, The Tuskegee Airmen*, Xenon Entertainment Group 1994

The crew of a crippled B-17 bomber waiting for their demise

On one of the many bombing missions over Germany during World War II, one of our B-17 bombers, while in formation with sixty other bombers, was hit by ground guns starting a fire in its third engine. The crippled bomber left the formation heading back to base, over 200 miles away. Soon it was alone, broadcasting a thick black smoke trail that could be seen over 50-miles from any direction as it slowly limped back toward home. But the crew knew their chances were slim for survival. Normally, a fire in a B-17 engine allows about 38 seconds before the plane blows up. But flames around the engine were not evident, simply bellows of black smoke billowing upward from the engine's oil, announcing to all German fighters that wounded prey was close.

Every man on the B-17 scanned the horizon with eagle eyes knowing their trailing plume of doom would soon bring in Nazi fighter planes to finish them off. Any black specks on the horizon, probably being an approaching German fighter, would indicate impending doom. The gunners in the B-17's turret guns were most diligent—even afraid to blink for fear of missing that dreaded approaching speck. No one in the ten-man crew spoke. The droning sound of the remaining three out-of-sync engines seemed like a meditation mantra.

"There! There it is! Three o'clock high!" shouted the top-turret gunner. All crew members turned to the starboard side of the bomber and noticed a speck above the horizon approaching at a high rate of speed. All turret guns fixed on the position. They waited as the speck grew to a dot, then a dot with wings. Still too far away to shoot, but first they must identify friend or foe. Larger and larger this incoming threat grew, but it had not yet opened fire on the B-17. Soon the fighter zoomed over the top of the bomber circling to the right in front of the wounded ship. The fighter had a red tail! It was a Tuskegee Airmen P-51 Mustang.

The B-17 's radio crackled, then came in clearly with a joking voice, "You Honkies lost?" The Tuskegee P-51 mustang fighter stayed with the B-17 and fought off all incoming enemy fighters pursuing the black smoke plume until the injured bomber arrived safely home. [41] What a wonderful way to developed TRUST among the whites.

The B-24 bomber crew of praying rednecks

The Tuskegee Airmen were, for the most part, kept a secret from the rest of

---

[41] The pilot of this B-17 wrote a letter to his mother describing this entire incident. I heard the letter read in its entirety while attending the Gaylord, Texas, Tuskegee Airmen National Convention in 2007.

the Army Air Corps. The Tuskegee Airmen were stationed in a secret base at Ramitelli on the eastern coast of Italy by the Adriatic Sea.

The point where the fighter escorts joined the bombers was called the rendezvous point. It was the fighter pilot's job to protect the bombers from enemy fighters trying to shoot them down. The bomber crews were concerned about the escort fighter planes punctuality arriving at the rendezvous point, for often the fighters got held up on other issues. This left our bombers without protection from our fighter escorts on their bombing run.

One day in the summer of 2013, I was giving a speech to the Kent, Ohio, Rotary Club about the Tuskegee Airmen. The speech was moving and covered the Tuskegee Airmen's accomplishments and secrecy, especially in protecting the bombers on all their bombing missions. When I was through speaking, an elderly Caucasian gentleman with white hair stood up. He had tears in his eyes. Our forthcoming conversation follows:

"Sir," I said, "I see you are upset. Did I say something in my speech that offended you?"

"No, Roger, you did not offend me. I must explain that I was a bomber pilot in World War Il," he sobbed, "and my entire crew consisted of Mississippi, Georgia, and Alabama rednecks. They hated blacks!" he declared. "However, despite that fact, every time we arrived at the rendezvous point, my entire crew dropped to their knees and prayed," he stated trying to hold back his tears.

"Did they pray that they would be kept safe on the bombing run?" I inquired.

"No, they did not," he replied.

"Did they pray they would be able to hit their targets without harming innocent civilians?" I inquired.

"No, they did not," he again stated.

"Sir, may I inquire why your redneck crew started to pray at the rendezvous point?" I queried.

"They prayed, that when their fighter escorts joined them, that they would have red tails," he exclaimed.

And with that I started to cry as well with at least half of the audience. What a meaningful moment for me. What a wonderful tribute to the Tuskegee Airmen. What a powerful trust these bomber crews had for these black Red Tails. These southern rednecks were prejudiced against blacks, but they trusted them with their lives.

THE VALUE OF MANAGING CONFLICT. The Tuskegee Airmen were not only in conflict with the Germans, but more often with the unfair treatment and discriminatory policies of the U.S. Army Air Corps. The Nazis wanted to destroy the U.S. Military, and many people in the U.S. Army Air Corps wanted to destroy the Tuskegee Airmen training program. Therefore, the Airmen had two enemies; they were fighting two wars, yet they responded to both their adversaries by always maintaining their dignity.

I greatly admired how the Tuskegee Airmen maintain the dignity of their adversaries while engaged in *conflict*. This amazing character trait prevailed while interacting with German military, prejudicial supervisors in the Army Air Corps, and detrimental treatment by civilians.

We will run out of fuel!

The Tuskegee Airmen were ordered to rendezvous with many B-17 bombers on March 24, 1944, about 125 miles south of Berlin for one of the major bombing runs expecting to end the war—Berlin. There was a major problem with this request. The Red Tails were stationed in Ramitelli, Italy. The P-51 Mustangs could not fly from Ramitelli to Berlin, over 1,600 miles round-trip, and have enough fuel left to get back to Ramitelli.[42] Their engines would quit somewhere over the Austrian Alps. When the Tuskegee Airmen pointed this out to their command, it seemed to fall on deaf ears. Sometimes the conflict between the Tuskegee Airmen and their white commanders was worse than their conflict with Germany.

The Tuskegee Airmen got wind of a railroad train shipment of P-51 underwing 110-gallon fuel tanks headed for a white military base near the boot of Italy. At 11:00 PM, on March 28, 1944, this train was intercepted by group of armed Tuskegee Airmen. It is important at this time to understand

---

the difference between "requisition" and "commandeer." There certainly wasn't time to requisition the P-51 underwing fuel tanks, so commandeer was a better option. A short time later, a freight train conducted by a little Italian man with frightened eyes the size of saucers, arrived at Ramitelli. The fuel tanks were unloaded and jerry-rigged under the wings of forty-three P-51 Red Tails. At 10:00 AM, under the command of Benjamin O. Davis, Jr., these Red Tails took off heading north to Germany.[43]

Is it stealing if fuel tanks owned by the U.S. Army Air Corps intended to be installed on their own P-51 Mustangs were taken by officers of the U.S. Army Air Corps and installed on P-51 Mustangs owned by the U.S. Army Air Corps? Is that not a peaceful and effective way of managing conflict?

Was the Berlin bombing mission successful? Well, the Germans had developed fighter jets called Me 262s, the world's first fighter jet. They used them against the Red Tails on this Berlin raid. The Tuskegee Airmen simply slowed down, and when the Me 262 jets zoomed passed them, the Airmen simply shot them down. Roscoe Brown was the first Tuskegee Airman to shoot down a jet. Two other jet fighters were shot down by redtail pilots. None of the Tuskegee Airmen were shot down or damaged.

Tuskegee Airmen were also trained as bomber pilots and crew

Back in the United States, additional Tuskegee Airmen were being trained as bomber pilots flying B-25 Mitchell bombers. It was the intention of the Army Air Corps and southern senators, congressmen, and military supervisors to see that this training program failed because of the incompetency of blacks—sound familiar?

Key Point

Some of the Tuskegee Airmen were raised by their grandparents, and many of these grandparents had parents who were slaves. If there is anything a slave learned quickly, it is how not to make a bad situation worse. This passive-response to injustice proved critically important to the success of the Airmen—a wonderful and effective way to handle conflict.

Commander Selway was assigned to the 477th MBG (Medium Bombardment Group). He was a bigot. He wanted the Tuskegee Airmen to fail. He refused to associate socially with black men and kept them

---

43 *Black Knights, The Story of the Tuskegee Airmen*, by Homan, Lynn and Reilly, Thomas, Pelican Publishing Company, 2001, Gretna, Louisiana

highly segregated. Selway wanted to show everyone how inadequate blacks could be. To help ensure their failure and low morale, the 477th MBG was moved from the Selfridge Field, Michigan base to Godman Army Field by Fort Knox, Kentucky.[44]

Godman Field was "...as close to hell as any place on earth," [45] [46] and too small to train the 477th and their B-25 bombers. The base had 1/7 the needed land area for bomber training, 1/5 the needed supply of gasoline, 1/4 the required hangar space, not enough runways, and much worse weather than the former Michigan base. All these insufficiencies were designed to ensure the Tuskegee Airmen bomber pilot training would be a failure.

In the town, the Tuskegee Airmen were not allowed to enter many restaurants, movie theaters, laundromats, or other public facilities. Clothing stores would sell clothes to the Tuskegee Airmen and Women but would not allow them to try on the clothes or shoes beforehand nor return them if they did not fit. They claimed white customers would not buy the clothing if they were worn by blacks.

On March 15, 1945, Colonel Selway moved the entire 477th MBG to Freeman Field in Seymour, Indiana, some think to further lower morale. The citizens of Seymour, Indiana, were very prejudiced. There were very few restaurants, stores, and theaters that would allow blacks to enter. Sunset laws encouraged blacks to be off the streets before dark. In Seymour, white military officers were taking captured German Nazi prisoners to the restaurants and theaters for recreation. The laundromats happily washed the German prisoners' clothes while refusing to allow the black Tuskegee officers use of the facility. The United States Army Air Corps was giving more rights and privileges to captured Nazi prisoners than to our own Tuskegee officers. [47]

You don't have to attend every argument you are invited to.
Thingsweforget.blogspot.com

---

44 From several personal interviews the author had with three original Tuskegee Airmen of the 477th MBG under the command of Selway: Lt. Arthur Saunders, Sgt. James Travis, and Major Edward Lunda from 2004 through 2007.
45 Ibid.
46 *Black Knights, The Story of the Tuskegee Airmen*, by Homan, Lynn and Reilly, Thomas, Pelican Publishing Company, 2001, Gretna. Louisiana
47 TIMELINE, Even Nazi prisoners of war in Texas were shocked at how black people were treated in the South, Heather Gilligan, October 26, 2017, https://timeline.com/nazi-prisoners-war-texas-f4a0794458ea

THE VALUE OF PRESERVING CHARACTER. (This is the basis for all the other heroic values; it is the most important.) One's *character* is determined by how one reacts to situations. Reacting negatively, positively, violently, peacefully, or not reacting at all to a bad situation is a personal choice and a true determination of one's character. Repeatedly acting positively to unfair and demeaning situations was an unwavering characteristic of the Tuskegee Airmen. I now realize that how I react to anything reveals to all who I am; it reveals to me who I am as well—I am my character. I continually witnessed the Tuskegee Airmen maintaining their quality of character while operating under demeaning circumstances.

As with other skills, repetition is required to maintain a high-level of efficiency. Fortunately, or unfortunately depending on your point-of-view, this world is filled with enough unpleasant people, confrontational individuals, and out-of-the-blue crisis situations to keep our "character" skills finely honed. Interacting positively with other Airmen, amiably interacting with the prejudicial Army Air Corps Commanders, and maintaining peaceful reactions to crisis situations (engine failures, accidents, enemy attacks, etc.) gave the Airmen plenty of practice.

There is a wonderful story about a Tuskegee Airmen that I have heard many times. It's part of the Tuskegee Airmen folklore and perfectly illustrates their very special character. I cannot verify its source. I will place myself in the story because it is easier to express by doing so.

About 55 years after WWII, I was in New York with a Tuskegee Airmen. He was about eighty years old and dressed in a suit and tie. We were walking down the sidewalk and came upon a rickety, old, newspaper stand managed by an overweight and unshaven proprietor wearing a torn, mustard-stained t-shirt. The Tuskegee Airmen went to the newspaper stand, took a Washington Post off the rack, and handed the disheveled proprietor a $1 bill. The Washington Post cost fifty cents at that time. The proprietor frowned at the Tuskegee Airmen, grabbed the $1 bill from his hands, and threw it into a cigar box full of change. He then took two quarters from the cigar box and, with a disgusted look on his face, threw them at the Airmen. The quarters bounced off the Airmen's chest and fell into the street gutter among some tobacco spit.

The Tuskegee Airmen reached into his suit coat pocket, pulled out a handkerchief, bent down into the gutter retrieving the quarters, and wiped them clean. He then turned to the nasty proprietor and said in a friendly voice, "Thank you, sir; you have a pleasant day." The Airmen then turned and continued walking down the sidewalk.

I watched this contemptible behavior in total dismay! I had just witnessed one of America's greatest war heroes be totally degraded. I then ran after the Airmen shouting, "How can you allow someone to treat you that way?! Where is your dignity? Where is your self-respect? Blacks always complain the way they are treated by whites; maybe it is because they allow it."

The Tuskegee Airmen stopped walking and turned around facing me. He gently tapped his finger on my chest as he stated with a pleasant voice and a warm twinkle in his eyes, "Roger, I decide how I behave, not him," pointing to the proprietor. "And I decide how I behave based on my values, on the kind of person I want to be, not on how others behave toward me."

I had accused this special man, this kind warrior, of not having any self-respect, of not having any dignity. As I quickly witnessed, he had more self-respect and dignity than anyone I had ever known! I was truly embarrassed. I was humiliated by my quick reactionary behavior. I was honored to have encountered a person with his extraordinary level of character.

In all the years I have associated myself with the Tuskegee Airmen, I have never seen any of them lose their temper, swear in anger, or degrade another person. They are, indeed, very endearing warriors.

Key Point

The Tuskegee Airmen knew that insulting those who were demeaning them would make them demeaning as well. The Tuskegee Airmen got up every morning with the desire to take complete charge, not over others, but over how they reacted to them.

THE VALUE OF NOT JUDGING OTHERS. The Tuskegee Airmen were always being negatively *judged*—they were accused of being lazy, incompetent, cowardly, and inept. Yet the Tuskegee Airmen did not judge those who were unfairly judging them. I was continuously amazed by how the Tuskegee Airmen kept from *judging* those who were negatively judging them.

The Tuskegee Airmen were not allowed to use the officer's club or athletic facilities.

The Uniform Code of Military Justice states that only officers are allowed in an officer's club. It does not make any mention of the officer's race, for when the Code was written, there were no black officers. In any case, because the Tuskegee Airmen were black, they were not allowed to enter the officer's club even though they were officers. When the Tuskegee Airmen tried to enter the officer's club at Freeman Field at Seymore, Indiana, they were denied entrance. Over the period of one week, sixty-one of them were arrested.

The Tuskegee Airmen were judged as undesirable to share a bar, a social club of camaraderie, and an athletic facility. How would the Tuskegee Airmen respond to this unfair judgment? Did they protest and riot? No. Did they write threatening letters to the base commander or report him to Washington D.C. military authorities? No. They secretly called a local newspaper reporter and snuck him on base to secretly watch what was happening.

Selway, the base commander, issued a document (Base Regulation 85-2) stating that all black officers knew they were not allowed in the white officer's club. All Tuskegee Airmen officers were ordered to sign this document, but 101 of them refused. Those 101 officers were arrested under article 64 of the Articles of War—refusing an order from a superior officer during time of war (punishable by death).

I want to pause here to emphasize this: The Tuskegee Airmen were charged with a crime punishable by death because they wanted to go into an officer's club and buy a beer. They were ordered to sign a document acknowledging they understood this. Well, they did not understand that; therefore, 101 refused to sign. Those who would not sign the document were charged with failure to obey an order during time of war. Of course, the war was in Europe.

The 101 arrested Airmen were flown to Godman Field and then transported in gray military POW (prisoner of war) transport vans to a prisoner-of-war camp at Fort Knox, Kentucky. Upon arrival at Fort Knox, the Airmen were met by seventy-five military police all armed with sub-machine guns. Walking around the compound, completely free and unescorted, were captured German prisoners-of-war all laughing at the Airmen. The Airmen were confined to barracks guarded by dogs and spotlights.

One of my friends, a member of the North Coast Chapter of the Tuskegee Airmen, was Major Edward Lunda. He was one of the 101 Tuskegee Airmen arrested for refusing to sign document 85-2. We were giving a speech together at a District Rotary Conference in Cleveland Ohio, where I mentioned he was charged with Article 64. Major Lunda stated he was never told that, but just arrested without any explanation and simply incarcerated in Fort Knox. He learned he was charged with Article 64 sixty-five years later by jointly giving a speech with me.

Another Tuskegee Airman who was among the 101 arrested was Coleman Alexander Young, who later became the mayor of Detroit, Michigan, serving as the first black mayor in Detroit from 1974 through 1994.

At the court-martial trial of the 101 Airmen, they were represented by a young attorney named Thurgood Marshall. If that name seems familiar to you, he later became a United States Supreme Court justice. Thurgood Marshall got all the 101 Airmen released, other than Roger Terri who brushed up against a provost marshal while entering the officer's club. He was charged with assault, found guilty, and fined $150.00.[48]

Despite all these obstacles placed in their path, their bomber training was successful. Their demonstrated skills as bomber pilots, chief engineers, bombardiers, and navigators were excellent.

Upon completion of their training, they were to be deployed in Europe to help replenish the large number of bomber losses suffered by the United States at the hands of Germany. As the 477th Medium Bombardment Group was ready for deployment, they were informed that none of the American fighting units overseas would accept them. They did not want blacks off their wings (history repeats itself). As a result, they were going to be sent to the Pacific Theater to operate as their own unit, but the atomic bomb was then dropped on Japan ending the war.[49]

What happened with the clandestine newspaper reporter? He was discovered by Commander Selway and kicked off the base, but not before he witnessed enough prejudice to write an exposing newspaper story that started a major investigation in Washington. Selway was transferred, and in 1948, President Truman created his executive order 9981 that desegregated the military. Blacks and whites would no longer be segregated in the barracks, the dining halls, and the officer's clubs.

President Clinton offers clemency to the 101 arrested Tuskegee Airmen

In 1995, President Bill Clinton in a ceremony in Atlanta, Georgia, offered clemency to the 101 arrested Airmen from their incarceration at Fort Knox and offered to clear their records of the incident if they individually requested. Some of the still-living 101 officers accepted President

---

48 Told to the author by Roger Terri.
49 Told to the author by his good friend Lieutenant Arthur Saunders, 477th Medium Bombardment Group, B-25 Mitchel Bomber, Original Tuskegee Airmen, 2007

Clinton's offer. Others wanted the arrest to stay on their records to show how ridiculously they were treated by the Army Air Corps.

On March 29, 2007, at the Gold Medal Ceremony in Washington D.C., I ran into Roger Terri on the steps of the Capital Building. I asked Roger Terri if President Clinton, in addition to clearing his record of his arrest and assault entering the officer's club, also returned the $150.00 he was fined. Roger Terri said, "Yes, he did, but I never saw it—he gave it to my wife."

Were there any black flight instructors?
White fighter pilots were sent home after 50 missions to become flight instructors at training bases. The Tuskegee pilots were never sent home because the U.S. Army Air Corps did not want black flight instructors.[50]

I am not aware of any black flight instructors at the Tuskegee Flying School in Alabama during the war. However, after the war, there were some. Tuskegee Airmen Col. Herbert Carter not only taught flying at Tuskegee but went overseas with other Airmen to teach German Pilots how to fly jets. How is that for not JUDGING others? [51]

Many Tuskegee Airmen flew over 100 missions. Tuskegee pilot Charles McGee flew 152 missions, and after flying in WW II, he flew in the Korean War and again in the Vietnam War totaling 6,100 flying hours and 409 combat missions, a record I believe is unbroken yet today (2021). [52] Colonel Charles McGee, now 100 years old, was promoted to brigadier general by President Trump at the State of the Union Address on February 4, 2020. He died on January 16, 2022, at the age of 102 inspiring years.

THE VALUE OF RECOGNIZING ACHIEVEMENTS. People who are unable to speak for themselves are rarely given *recognition*. People in positions of authority often receive and even take the recognition for the deeds of those serving under them. The Tuskegee Airmen gave recognition to those responsible for their accomplishments regardless of who they were —friend or foe.

I had a strong need to comprehend where the Tuskegee Airmen, in this case Benjamin O. Davis Jr., developed his remarkable recognition of another's skills in correcting the injustices and supporting the achieve-

---

50 Told to the author by Lt. Herbert E. Carter and his wife Mildred Carter at their home in Tuskegee, Alabama 2007
51 Told to the author by Herbert Carter during my stay at this house in Tuskegee, Alabama in March of 2006.
52 BET — Black Entertainment Television, Colonel Charles McGee USAF (Ret.), https://www.bet.com/topics/c/colonelcharles-mcgee-usaf-ret.html, 2018

ments of those unable to speak for themselves. I learned of many other examples of this fine characteristic to help guide my research.

Did the civilian community embrace the Tuskegee Airmen after the war?

After the war was over and the black servicemen were sent home, their homecomings were often brutal and cruel. The NAACP reported that 1946 was ". . . one of the grimmest years in the history of the organization," Despite the promises of post-war equality, many black servicemen were greeted with waves of lynchings, eye-gouging, and blowtorch killings! [53]

Do not tell your children you were a Tuskegee Airman

To protect their children from ridicule at school, many Tuskegee Airmen never told their children they were war heroes, aircraft mechanics, bomber pilots, or fighter-plane pilots. After all, there were no black pilots in the military, the military was segregated, and everyone knew this. Those Tuskegee Airmen who did share their accomplishment with their children often found it to be a mistake. Their children went to school bragging about their fathers' heroic accomplishments during the war. They were beat up by their peers and sent home from school by their teachers for lying. There were no black pilots! There were no black aircraft mechanics! There were no black aircraft controllers. All the children were liars and needed to be taught a lesson.

One Tuskegee Airmen, James Travis, was assigned to B-25 bombers and a member of the 477th Medium Bombardment Group. After the war, he never told his son what he had done in the war or any of his activities. He did not want his son to suffer because of the prejudice and confusion about the Tuskegee Airmen. When his son was almost sixty-five years old, James Travis took an old photograph of himself in a Tuskegee Airmen uniform and left it to be discovered on an end table in his living room. His son, while visiting, eventually found it. Shortly afterwards, James Travis walked into his living room to find his son holding the small photograph with a stunned look on his face. Looking up at his father he said, "Dad, you were a Tuskegee Airmen?!!!" That evening a long conversation took place explaining this family secret. It was difficult for the son to understand, at sixty-five years of age, that his father was a war hero. [54]

---

53 *Red-Tail Angels, The Story of the Tuskegee Airmen of WWII*, page 121, Patricia and Frederick McKissack, Walker Publishing Company, 1995
54 Told to the author many times by his friend, Tuskegee Airmen James Travis

During the war, Hitler, after receiving criticism from the United States about his treatment of the Jews, rebutted by saying, "My treatment of the Jews is no worse than the United States military's treatment of their own black officers![55]

Learning to circumnavigate prejudice in the military prepared many for civilian life

Shaker Heights is a suburb of Cleveland, Ohio. In the 1950s, Shaker Heights was a high middle-class city that was all white. I know this; I grew up in Shaker Heights.

The first black man to live in Shaker Heights was a Tuskegee Airmen named Ted Mason. The architect he hired to design and build his house was a Tuskegee Airmen named Arthur Saunders of the 477 MBG (Medium Bombardment Group). Arthur Saunders knew that homes built in Shaker Heights had to be approved by the City of Cleveland Architecture Review Board. Saunders also knew that Ted Mason's house plans would not be approved if it was known that he or his architect were black.

When it came time to appear before at the Architecture Review Board in Cleveland, Arthur Saunders hired a white architect to represent him. Ted Mason was not required to appear. The same technique was used to obtain a zoning permit and a building permit. Well what do you know? Ted Mason's house plans were approved. His house was built without Ted Mason or Arthur Saunders appearing on the property.

Upon near completion of the house, both Ted Mason and Arthur Saunders went to inspect the home. The appearance of two black men, especially in business suits, caused quite a reaction in the neighborhood. Shortly after their arrival at the house, the neighbors came out in droves inquiring what two black men were doing on the property. The crowd quickly grew in numbers. The Shaker Heights police were called. After the police arrived, spokespersons for the crowd informed the police that the neighborhood was simply trying to protect their property, that these two black men might be burglars or intruders. They certainly did not have any right to be on the property.

Ted Mason quickly identified himself as the owner of the home showing the approved plans from the Architectural Review Board from the City of Cleveland. Art Saunders identified himself as the architect. The police disbursed the crowd informing all that the two mysterious black men were legitimate, and that a black family, for the first time, had just moved into Shaker Heights. What a recognized achievement that was.

---

55 President George W. Bush, Congressional Gold Medal Ceremony, the Rotunda, Washington D.C., March 29, 2007

I remember being ten years old and listening to my father say during the dinner table conversation that a black family had finally moved into Shaker Heights. I had no idea that I would be writing about the event with great pride sixty years later.

Art Saunders has told me many times that being a Tuskegee Airmen taught him how to use unjust laws to beat an unfair system. Saunders did so many times while part of the 477th MBG, using the Uniform Code of Military Justice to fight prejudice against the Tuskegee Airmen. [56]

REVERING THESE VALUES. People often give up some of their values when they do not receive positive results. But the Tuskegee Airmen, despite unfair and unjust criticism, and despite few rewards for their virtues, continued employing their values because of who they wanted to be, because of who they were.

I admired how the Tuskegee Airmen maintained their values for seventy years, not to please someone else, but to honor the unfaltering principles within them. To my knowledge, none of the 14,000 Tuskegee Airmen has ever been arrested for a felony. I discovered, through repeated examples, that these special values were ingrained in the Tuskegee Airmen's nature, and not just occurring in a few isolated instances.

You have just read about several events occurring in the Tuskegee Airmen's history. I recognized many outstanding character values in their repeated behavior as they peacefully interacted with others who were trying to discredit them. I selected the Airmen's values that particularly interested me, exceptional values that I observed with the Airmen through my studies and countless interactions with them, although I am sure there are many more. I researched over one hundred degrading-crisis situations the Airmen endured. I repeatedly found that the Tuskegee Airmen used many of these fourteen values and the associated actions as a basis for peaceful interaction. Thousands of Tuskegee Airmen raised all over the United States under different conditions seemed to behave uniformly. No wonder I was so inspired.

The Tuskegee Airmen were kept a secret after the war

Because of the Tuskegee Airmen's incredible success, they were kept a secret after the war. By doing so, they did not embarrass the white military leaders, congressmen, and other government officials that were initially so vocal about their impending failure and incompetence. By the government keep-

---

56 Tuskegee Airmen Arthur Saunders frequently told the author this story. We gave over thirty speeches together representing the North Coast Chapter of the Tuskegee Airmen and he told this story about Ted Mason at each speech.

ing the blacks' accomplishments hidden from white society after WWII, blacks would tend to remain in lower social levels encouraging the prejudice and discrimination against them to continue. If the Tuskegee Airmen's heroic accomplishments were widely known, especially their role in saving thousands of white military personnel, the government and military would have to, somehow, justify their cruel and unfair treatment of these amazing heroes. Therefore, after WWII, the records of the Tuskegee Airmen were classified and sequestered for twenty-five years to hide their success.[57]

Another secret kept about the Tuskegee Airmen

At the near beginning of Chapter 1, I was discussing the 250 inner-city kids I brought to Hiram College from the City of Cleveland to see the movie The Tuskegee Airmen. You may remember after showing the film, I had 250 angry teenage children on my hands. For fear of redundancy, I would like to repeat why they were angry.

> For years you white folks have been demanding that we blacks try harder to get along with you, but you whites never told us how to do this. Here, in the movie we just saw, the Tuskegee Airmen showed us how. The secrets about getting along with whites, or blacks, or with anybody for that matter, was demonstrated and understood by these blacks, the Tuskegee Airmen, not the whites. The Tuskegee Airmen are our heroes too, black heroes for black kids, yet they were kept a secret from us. Why?

How ironic it is for me, a white man, to have discovered the secret of blacks getting along with whites in the hearts of the black Tuskegee Airmen. In our society, black children desperately need black heroes of peace.

The Tuskegee Airmen's records were available after the twenty-five of sequestering. The word about the Airmen gradually started to spread through the efforts of the emerging Tuskegee Airmen Chapters throughout the United States started by Lt. Col. Alexander Jefferson in 1972. But the Tuskegee Airmen were promoted primarily by their heroic accomplishments, not by their problem-solving values of peace. Hopefully, this book will help serve that purpose.

Sadly, Jefferson died in Detroit, Michigan on June 22, 2022. He was 100 years old. He is a true legend. He was my dear friend.

---

57 From a personal interview with my friend Edith Roberts, female Tuskegee Airmen pilot and wife of Spanky Roberts, original Tuskegee Airmen, 2010.

The nation's first Top Gun!

The United States Air Force was formed on September 18, 1947 by President Truman. It was fully integrated. On May 2, 1949, the United States Air Force held its first gunnery competition, the USAF Worldwide Fighter Gunnery Meet, started sixty miles northwest of Las Vegas, Nevada, at an area called Frenchman Flats. The competition was divided into two categories—jets and propeller-driven fighter planes—and consisted of aerial gunnery, dive-bombing, skip-bombing, and rocketry. The Tuskegee Airmen were represented by their best gunners from the 332nd Fighter Group flying P-47 Thunderbolts, the same plane that was used to attack the German Destroyer in Trieste Harbor, Yugoslavia. The Tuskegee pilots were Lt. Halbert Alexander, Lt. James Harvey, Capt. Alva Temple, and Lt. Harry Stewart. [58]

Well, the Tuskegee Airmen of the 332nd Fighter Group won first place for the entire event. After the finish of the competition and before the next-day awards ceremony, the 332nd were given some rest-and-relaxation time. In their uniforms, all pressed and polished, they entered the first-class Las Vegas hotel where the award ceremonies were to be held the next day. Being black, they were immediately escorted out of the hotel by security guards shouting, "KEEP MOVING!"

On May 12, 1949, at the same hotel that ejected the black Tuskegee Airmen the previous day, a thirty-six-inch trophy was presented to the four pilots of the 332nd. The trophy was to stay on display at the Pentagon and engraved with the name of a new winner every two years. Shortly after the ceremony, the trophy disappeared. Vanished! Someone did not want blacks to win the first top gun. Again, the Tuskegee Airmen's accomplishments were being kept a secret. The four winning pilots addressed this situation with calm dignity. They wanted to maintain the very high values of their fellow warriors of peace.

Forty-five years later, one Ms. Zellie Orr found the missing trophy in a remote storage area at the Historical Museum at Wright-Patterson AFB in Dayton, Ohio. This trophy was transferred to the Tuskegee Airmen Museum in Detroit, Detroit City Airport, Main Hangar, Michigan, where it was presented to Col. Stewart, one of the winning pilots, and to the relatives of the Tuskegee pilot winners at a dinner ceremony on December 10, 2004. I was at that ceremony and was deeply moved.

---

58 *Tuskegee Airmen, The First Top Guns "The Last Hurrah"* 2004 Harry Stewart Lt. Col. USAF Retired

In autumn of 1994, Col. William Campbell of the USAF was looking through the current edition of the USAF Almanac. Campbell was looking up the winners of all the USAF Fighter Gunnery Meets starting with the first. The winner of the initial 1949 Las Vegas Gunnery Meet was listed as "Unknown.[59] Will this prejudice never end?

How do other heroes of peace behave?

Discovered from my research, here are the rich values and heroic actions the Tuskegee Airmen have left the world. Here are the tools for peacefully running our companies, for patiently raising our children, for compassionately governing our families, for efficiently managing our schools, for enriching our personal relationships, and for granting our governments the authority to safeguard us through peace.

Key Point

My research identified fourteen values that are found in the hearts of most good people everywhere, not only in my eighty chosen heroes of peace. What makes these values so unique in my selected heroes is how these heroes would apply these values in solving a crisis peacefully. The heroic explanation of each value is not the dictionary's definition of the word, but rather describes the heroes' methodology for practicing the value. The explanation of the value is worded as the action necessary to apply the value as a hero of peace. As an example, let's look at the value of courage: The action used by my selected heroes to apply the value of courage is to honor, respect, and welcome fear, for only fear can offer you an opportunity to demonstrate courage.

---

59 Ibid

**THE DECISION-MAKING VALUES OF THE HEROES OF PEACE
AND THE TUSKEGEE AIRMEN**

1. Choosing Behavior

Govern yourself by never allowing another's behavior to negatively influence your conduct. Your actions are always your responsibility; they are never another's fault. Determine your behavior from your values, from the kind of person you want to be—never from how others behave toward you.

2. Creating Change

Encourage positive change, not through criticism, but through your continuous achievements and examples of excellence for all to witness. When criticized by others, offer continual examples of excellence as your only response.

3. Developing Vision

Envision things as wonderful as they can be, not as they are, and then strive to create positive change toward these envisioned goals. All great accomplishments started as a vision that others could not see.

4. Overcoming Obstacles

Realize that obstacles are not barriers to your goals, but opportunities for growth and challenges to enrich your self-confidence by mastering new skills. A person having reached a goal without overcoming obstacles has learned nothing and accomplished even less. Conquered obstacles are the only qualifying credentials of heroes and a measure of your commitment and leadership.

5. Sustaining Self-esteem

Enhance your self-esteem, not from the opinions of others, but from the compassionate causes you have chosen to embrace, and the perseverance and courage expended toward their resolve.

6. Displaying Compassion

Give simply to increase the amount of goodness in the world—often without recognition or reward. Give more to others than you receive in return, and carefully sustain this inequity as a distinctive characteristic of your leadership.

7. Addressing Courage

Honor, respect, and welcome fear, for only fear can offer you an opportunity to demonstrate courage.

8. Perseverance

Never give up. Most perceived failures are not failures at all, but instead successfully completed steppingstones toward a goal. The only time you can fail is if you quit pursuing your goals.

9. Encouraging Trust

Honor all commitments and obligations to everyone, especially yourself. Your pledge should be as meaningful to a king as to a beggar, for the value of a commitment is determined from its source, not to whom it is directed.

10. Managing Conflict

While engaging your adversaries, always maintain their dignity. This is the only road to lasting peace.

11. Preserving Character

How you react to any incident not only determines your true character, but boldly announces to all onlookers who you are. Therefore, courageously fulfill the obligations of being human by revering all life, defending the righteous, promoting peace, spreading compassion, rendering joy, and sharing your assets* with those less fortunate.

12. Judging Others

Observe, but never judge. Seek out the differences in others and then celebrate them, for such diversity** is the true potpourri of humanity and will enrich you with the knowledge and wisdom of the human experience.

13. Recognizing Achievements

Serve enthusiastically as a spokesperson for the accomplishments and concerns of others. Attentive leaders crusade for the issues, ideas, and achievements of those less able to speak for themselves giving ample recognition for their origin.

14. Revering these Values

Uphold this Value System, especially under adverse conditions, not to please someone else, but to honor the unfaltering principles within you, to validate your character as the type of person you want to be, and to gradually realize the awesome potential of being human.

*assets = One's strength, capacity to help, capacity to protect, capacity to defend, and capacity to rescue. One's abilities, education, talents, insight, wisdom, labor, knowledge, wealth, belongings, property, and any similar thing that can be utilized to bring benefit to another.

**diversity = one's abilities, interests, talents, experiences, beliefs, customs, culture, points-of-view, rituals, influences, networks, assets, and any beneficial characteristic distinguishing one person from another.

If you think I am implying that heroes of peace seem to harbor these special values that others might not possess, well, you are correct. I am also implying that these special values are nearly universal in peaceful heroes all over the world, regardless of the heroes' gender, age, religion, ethnicity, culture, wealth, or poverty.

Do Heroes of Peace have a different brain structure?

Is there really a difference in the brain structure or function of peaceful heroes compared to the brains of non-hero types? Dr. Abigail Marsh, a neuroscientist at Georgetown University, ran experiments on the brains of known heroes selected from Carnegie Heroes[60] recipients. For a good contrast, Marsh also studied and compared the brains of psychopaths. She studied the amygdala—two, tiny, almond-shaped sections of the brain that are the integrative center for emotions, emotional behavior, and motivations.[61] The amygdala subconsciously recognizes danger and reacts faster than conscious thought.[62] Marsh found that the amygdalas in the brains of heroes were larger and reacted faster and with more intensity than the smaller and slower reacting amygdalas in the brains of psychopaths.[63] When heroes observe serious danger affecting the safety of another, they often react immediately, without thinking, without regard to consequences, as their larger amygdalas instantly triggers their reaction—much as our hand immediately reacts when touching a hot stove.[64] Heroes with larger amygdalas are also the type of person who would donate a kidney to a perfect stranger. Such heroes are the type of my eighty heroic persons I have studied while discovering their heroic values. Psychopaths, with their smaller amygdalas, are usually much slower to react to danger affecting the safety of someone else, if they respond at all.

Are heroes of peace made or born? Do war heroes, policemen, paramedics, or firemen have larger amygdalas? Are people with larger amygdalas, in addition to instantly coming to the aid of others, also kinder, gentler, more patient and understanding that those with smaller amygdalas? Is it reasonable to assume that individuals born with the abilities for extreme love and kindness would naturally evolve into heroes of peace? There is much research that needs to be done. If a black person living in a time of extreme hate

60 The Carnegie Hero Fund Commission, also known as Carnegie Hero Fund, was established to recognize persons who perform extraordinary acts of heroism in civilian life in the United States and Canada.
61 https://nba.uth.tma.edu>neuroscience
62 Carnegie Heroes and the Neuroscience Behind the Acts of Heroism—Scott Pelley meets with Carnegie Hero Fund awardees and reports on a possible difference in brain make-up for those who commit heroic acts. November 7, 2021,
63 Scott Pelley, 60 Minutes, "Carnegie Heroes and the Neuroscience Behind Acts of Heroism," November 7, 2021
64 Ibid

and prejudice would volunteer to place his or her life in danger and fight to protect the lives and safety of those who hated him, would that suggest he had a larger amygdala? Would this be true of my eighty heroes of peace?

What is a hero?

Heroes of peace, without regard to personal consequences, embrace obstacles as opportunities for growth, utilize fear as a means to show courage, protect and maintain the dignity of their adversaries, crusade compassionately for those unable to fight for themselves, and celebrate diversity for the enrichment of mankind. According to the Carnegie Heroes' Fund Commission[65], a hero is "a man or woman that willingly and knowingly risk their lives to an extraordinary degree to save or attempt to save the life of another human being."

Am I not destroying my enemies when I make friends of them?
Abraham Lincoln

Do not ask what you expect from life, but rather ask
what life expects from you.
Viktor E. Frankl

As we let our own light shine, we unconsciously give other people
permission to do the same.
Nelson Mandela

---

65 The two-fold mission of the Carnegie Hero Fund Commission founded in 1904: "To recognize and support those who perform acts of heroism in civilian life in the United States and Canada." See https://www.carnegiehero.org

Key Point

Humans have the gift of "intentional free choice." Is this good or bad? Well, it depends on how humans use their intentional free choice—to protect or control, to rescue or enslave, to love or to hate, to improve or neglect. Possessing intentional free choice requires humans to be accountable for their behavior—it created the reality of right and wrong, it made humans responsible for their decisions.

Humans utilize intentional free choice to express their unique ability for love, charity, compassion, and sacrifice for the benefit of another. Humans also utilize free choice to intentionally improve themselves through education and acquiring new skills, "to decide what kind of person they want to be, and then actually create that individual."

Free choice also empowers humans to intentionally demonstrate hate, greed, indifference, neglect, and violence. Therefore, "free choice" can manifest a great benefit or a dreaded consequence. Free choice, for it to be beneficial, must be guided by a positive value system enriched with compassion. "Free choice," without positive guidance, is chaos riding on the wind.

If people do not intentionally guide their free-choice decisions with a positive value system, free choice may be guided by their instincts. Animals have little free choice and kill instinctually; humans have free choice and kill and destroy intentionally.

The above paragraph gives my discovered Heroes' Value System its true significance, for its importance in positively guiding our intentional free choices cannot be over emphasized.

III. How I Came to Know and Admire the Tuskegee Airmen

Excellence is to do a common thing in an uncommon way.
Booker T. Washington

The cultural effect of the Tuskegee Airmen's values and positive be-havior was not realized by many of the Airmen. As hundreds of the Airmen have told me, they were assigned a job and were doing it as best as they could. None of the many Airmen I interviewed consider themselves a hero. My discovery of the Airmen's values and their peaceful crisis-man-agement solutions was a long and involved journey laced with inspirations and epiphanies. I went to their weekly meetings, attend their programs for the public, joined their presentations at schools, created and taught courses about them at four colleges, and participated in their annual conventions. To assist my research, I gave speeches about the Airmen all over the coun-try. I wanted the Airmen to hear what I had discovered about them. I needed these experts to comment on my findings. This chapter addresses how I was accepted by this wonderful society of Tuskegee heroes, and how I obtained sufficient knowledge about Tuskegee Airmen to write this book.

Discovering the thought process used by the Tuskegee Airmen when faced with a crisis

I was very inspired after the Tuskegee Airmen left the meeting at Hiram College. I said goodbye with thanks to the 250 inner-city school chil-dren (Chapter One). I was determined to learn more about the Tuskegee Airmen, to research them, to try to find a methodology to their crisis-solv-ing thought process. This seemed very unlikely at first, for how could the values of 14,000 people from all over the United States be almost the same? How could their thought processes in a crisis be nearly uniform? These remarkable values and coping skills were certainly not taught to the Tuskegee Airmen from the United States Army Air Corps.

Today, when someone is insulted, degraded, and unfairly treated, they often respond with aggression, retaliation, lawsuits, and revenge. When the Tuskegee Airmen were insulted, degraded, and treated unfairly, they often responded passively to keep the prejudicial situation from escalating. Any strong retaliation or aggressive behavior from the Tuskegee Airmen would be addressed with expulsion, court martial, or closure of the entire Tuskegee flying program.

How I got to know the Tuskegee Airmen

In 2003, I joined the Cleveland North Coast Chapter of the Tuskegee Airmen as a volunteer. In 2008, I was elected chapter president—being the first (if not only) male, Caucasian president of a Tuskegee Airmen chapter in the United States. I attended many national Tuskegee Airmen events to broaden my understanding of their rich culture. I was researching to learn how the Tuskegee Airmen utilized their amazing ability to peacefully solve problems created by those trying to degrade them and destroy their flying program.

I attended numerous events:

Detroit City Airport for the "Top Gun" trophy ceremony on December 10, 2004

Molten Field in Tuskegee, Alabama for the Field Restoration Dedication

Omaha, Nebraska, for the August 2004 Tuskegee Airmen National Convention

The Tuskegee Airmen Recognition Ceremony, March of 2006, Tuskegee University, Tuskegee, Alabama.

Southwest Airlines dedication of one passenger jet with the Tuskegee Airmen logo

Capitol Building Rotunda in Washington D.C. for the Congressional Gold Medal presentations with President Bush on March 29, 2007

Inauguration of President Barack Obama in Washington D.C. with the Tuskegee Airmen on January 20, 2009

I started giving speeches and seminars about the Tuskegee Airmen's values all around the United States, especially at military bases and national Tuskegee Airmen conventions. Some of the speeches and seminars that I presented are in the Appendix. My programs, speeches, college classes, and Tuskegee Airmen interviews continued into 2015.

As the years passed, I met and interviewed many original Tuskegee Airmen and Women who were eager to share their stories and who were interested in their value system that I discovered through my years of research. That last sentence seems a little odd. Do I really mean that the Tuskegee Airmen, themselves, were not aware of the Value System I discovered about them? Do I really mean to imply that the Tuskegee Airmen did not know the legacy they left the human race? Yes, that is what I mean to say.

I presented the Tuskegee Airmen's Values and methodologies to the Tuskegee Airmen

At the Tuskegee Airmen Convention in Philadelphia in July of 2008, I gave a luncheon speech to a group of around 125 people that mostly consisted of original Tuskegee Airmen and their relatives. In my speech, I talked solely about my discovery of the Tuskegee Airmen Value system. I knew my speech was new material. I knew it was a revolutionary discovery that I hoped would be met with acceptance. I covered in detail every attribute: Behavior, Change, Vision, Obstacles, Self-esteem, Compassion, Courage, Perseverance, Trust, Conflict, Character, Judging, and Recognition. Was I greeted with a standing ovation and deafening applause after my speech? No, I received total silence. Not one clap from anyone. I looked out over the audience and noticed many of the Tuskegee Airmen had a confused look on their face and were earnestly whispering to each other. I overheard those conversations closest to the speaker's podium:

"Did we really do all that?"

"I never looked at our accomplishments in that way, have you?"

"I guess we did do those things, it makes sense to me now."

"We were just doing what we had to do."

"All we did was follow orders, just like we were expected to do."

"This can't be something new because we did these things sixty years ago!"

"What's going on here? We have always been called heroes just for doing our job—now this!"

"What a refreshing and meaningful new way of looking at our legacy!"

"I guess we did do those things; I guess we did."

Suddenly, after about thirty seconds of total silence, everyone rose to their feet cheering and applauding. What a delayed reaction, but as you can see, I view the Tuskegee Airmen's legacy quite differently from others. I am so excited about the Tuskegee Airmen's true legacy, so overwhelmed by what they can teach us about peaceful problem resolution, that I have, so far, dedicated over twenty years of my life to researching the Tuskegee Airmen and writing this book so their legacy will be preserved and available for all in the future. I have not only researched these discovered values but taught them to hundreds of students in my classes at Hiram College. I reviewed hundreds of inputs from my students throughout the years on what values worked and those that were more difficult. I smoothed out misunderstandings, tweaked wording for clearer understandings, and read hundreds of research papers on the Tuskegee Airmen and other heroes of peace.

The Congressional Gold Medal Ceremony in Washington D.C.

It was announced several months in advance that the Tuskegee Airmen were going to receive the Congressional Gold Medal from President George W. Bush in March of 2007. Because I was the president of the North Coast Chapter of the Tuskegee Airmen, I was sent many emails regarding the event. Some of the emails pointed out that each Tuskegee Airmen would have to pay $42.00 to cover the cost of their medal. Forms were sent to me and to the Tuskegee Airmen for sending in the advanced payment. It appeared to me that this was a slap-in-the-face kind of award ceremony, honoring these great people with the understanding if an individual Airman did not pay his/her $42.00, then he/she would not receive the Congressional Gold Medal. This not only infuriated me, but fortunately infuriated an anonymous benefactor who, three days before the award ceremony, purchased all the Congressional Gold Medals for the Tuskegee Airmen and had them waiting at the ceremony site. I saw the box containing all the medals just outside the Capitol rotunda. Tuskegee Airmen were asked to make sure they took one out of the box after the ceremony.

On March 29, 2007, over 300 surviving Tuskegee Airmen were called to Washington D.C. to receive the Congressional Gold Medal for their great service to this country. The ceremony was held in the Capitol Building Rotunda—under the dome. President George Bush, Former Secretary of Defense Colin Powell, Speaker of the House Nancy Pelosi, Senators Carl Levin and Mitch McConnell, and Representative Charles Rangel were a few of the dignitaries present.

I was among about 100 Caucasians who were unknowingly sitting in seats that had been reserved for the Tuskegee Airmen's families, all of whom were in another area getting their photograph taken with President Bush. Shortly, Representative Charles Rangel approach our group, and with a chuckle in his voice said, "These seats are reserved for the Tuskegee Airmen family members. Any of you white folks who are not relatives of the Tuskegee Airmen, please move to the rear of the room where you may stand by the televisions cameras." With that, all 100 of us arose and went to the rear of the room. Most of us were laughing.

The Congressional Gold Medal Ceremony was a very respectful and warming tribute to the Tuskegee Airmen. Some of the speakers' more poignant remarks I have transcribed below.

Representative Charles Rangel

Nobody white or black in this country can understand how God has given you so much courage, from a nation that has rejected you because of your color, said you couldn't fight, said you couldn't fly, said you just weren't worthy, and you had to go out and prove to them just how wrong they were! And how tragic it was to see that the very enemy that you fought, after you came back to this great country, to see how German prisoners of war, were treated better than you were on your return.

Senator Mitch McConnell

The Tuskegee Airmen fought for a country that didn't want them in combat. . . . Thank you for leaving our country better than you found it.

Senator Carl Levin

It is the ultimate act of patriotism to love your country even when that love is not reciprocated. So, when a special love of country exists when one must suspend a sense of anger and resist feelings of despair to fight for the right to fight, perhaps to die in defense of, a nation many of whose citizens and institutions are denigrating your very humanity. What is it that those young men saw in our nation which drove them to defend it in face of the pain inflicted upon them by laws promoting segregation and practices reflecting racism? They must have sensed, that despite the bigotry, that this was a nation worth fighting for. They must have seen a spark of hope that this was a country worth dying for . . . and thank God they did!

President George W. Bush

Having just come from taking photographs with the Tuskegee Airmen in the rotunda, I am impressed that I am among heroes who are not statues, but among heroes who still live. . . . I thank you for the honor that you have brought to our country, and the medal you are about to receive means that our country honors you. . . . Even the

Nazis asked why a group of men would fight for a country that treated them so unfairly? ...The Tuskegee Airmen felt a sense of urgency, for they were fighting two wars. One took place in Europe, and the other in the hearts and minds of our citizens. They not only fought for us on the battlefield, but they fought for the entire soul of this nation.

Thank you for not giving up on the promise of America. ... It is not often that one gets to meet the guys that have paved the path for you. ...The Tuskegee Airmen helped win a war and help change a nation for the better. Yours is a story of the human spirit, and it ends like all great stories do, with wisdom and lessons and hope for tomorrow. The medal that we give you today means we are doing our small part to insure that your story will be told and honored for generations to come, and I would like to offer a gesture for all the unreturned salutes and unforgivable indignities, and so, on behalf of the office that I hold and the country that honors you, I salute you!

Having said that, President Bush stood at attention and saluted the 300 Tuskegee Airmen in the room. I then watched as all the Tuskegee Airmen stood up and returned the president's salute. It was a heart-warming and beautiful moment. Tuskegee Airmen red tail pilot Lee Archer later commented about the president's salute, "The debt has been paid!"

Some incidental Tuskegee Airmen histories

In 1964, blacks were given the right to vote without paying a poll tax. 1982 was the first year there were no reported lynchings in United States. In 1973 there was a Tuskegee Airmen Chapter convention in Washington, D.C.—only one year after Alexander Jefferson had the first Airmen meet-

ing at his house.[66] The first movie called "The Tuskegee Airmen" was released by HBO in 1995 and shown only on television.

---

66 Col. Alexander Jefferson, one of the endorsers of this book, P-51 red-tail pilot, told this to the author many times from 2004 through 2008

Benjamin O. Davis Jr. died at 89 years of age on July 4, 2002, at Walter Reed Army Medical Center in Washington, D.C. General Davis was buried at Arlington National Cemetery. A Red Tail P-51 Mustang flew overhead during his funeral services.

Bill Clinton said, "General Davis is here today as proof that a person can overcome adversity and discrimination, achieve great things, turn skeptics into believers; and through example and perseverance, one person can bring truly extraordinary change."

A Movie

The first theater-released movie about the Tuskegee Airmen, entitled *Red Tails*, was made by director George Lucas in 2012. When I heard that George Lucas was making a theater movie about the Tuskegee Airmen, I wrote him a letter trying to emphasize the incredible opportunity he had at his fingertips and the unbelievable honor and valor of the Airmen. I encouraged Lucas to learn about the Tuskegee Airmen's coveted courage and fearlessness first, then make the movie afterwards.

March 8, 2007
Mr. George Lucas
Lucasfilm Ltd.
PO Box 2009
San Rafael, CA 94912

Dear George Lucas:

The Tuskegee Airmen and Women practiced a set of values, problem-solving abilities, and conflict-resolution techniques that, if employed in our businesses and taught in our schools, would literally enrich our nation's future with integrity, prosperity, and peace.

By owning the rights to produce the Tuskegee Airmen movie, you control a medium for providing these powerful principles to positively influence our struggling youth. You supervise a means for presenting these enriching values to empower our schools, families, and corporations with the ability to conquer obstacles through peaceful means.

You are in a unique position harboring an awesome potential. Please, for the needed enlightenment of our youth, for the inspiration of the American people, and for the peaceful prosperity of our nation's future, do not accept a Tuskegee Airmen script containing anything less than I described above.

To further understand these remarkable abilities, I have enclosed an outline of a Tuskegee Airmen curriculum I teach at Hiram College describing these extraordinary attributes in more detail.

Sincerely,
Roger F. Cram
Member and spokesperson, The Tuskegee Airmen,
North Coast Chapter

I received a form-letter answer from Lucas thanking me for my interest. As it turned out, the movie *Red Tails* was not spectacular, was rated only 40% by Rotten Tomatoes, was not a factual account of the Tuskegee Airmen, and took in $6.6 million less than its production budget. [67] However, the more publicity about the Tuskegee Airmen that reached the public the better. The glory of the Tuskegee Airmen was slowly being revealed.

Closing Thought

Meeting and getting to know the Tuskegee Airmen has been one of the enriching highlights of my life. Hearing their stories, studying their accomplishments, learning their values, and trying to understand their pain and frustrations has been life changing for me.

Almost every Tuskegee Airmen I met has become a friend. I am slowly—and sadly—watching them die. I am experiencing the end of a wonderful era.

On Tuesday, September 27, 2022, the day I finished writing this book, I inserted two one-dollar bills into a vending machine offering diet Cokes for $1.75. A diet Coke and a quarter were returned to me. The coin was a new 2021 quarter depicting the Tuskegee Airmen National Historic Site in Alabama. I smiled. Serendipity, sitting on my shoulder, smiled as well.

---

67   Red Tails, en.wikipedia.org

The only time we can fail is if we quit. Most perceived failures are only stepping-stones we encounter along the path to a goal. Obstacles are opportunities for growth; therefore, encourage and embrace them.
Arthur Saunders—Tuskegee Airman

Freedom is not worth having if it does not connote freedom to err. It passes my comprehension how human beings…can delight in depriving other human beings of that precious right.
Mahatma Gandhi

There are only two ways of living your life. One is as though nothing is a miracle. The other is as if everything is a miracle.
Albert Einstein

Chapter Two

The Values of Behavior, Creating Change, and Recognizing the Achievements of Others

Choosing Behavior

Govern yourself by never allowing another's behavior to negatively influence your conduct. Your actions are always your responsibility; they are never another's fault. Determine your behavior from your values, from the kind of person you want to be—never from how others behave toward you.

Creating Change

Encourage positive change, not through criticism, but through your continuous achievements and examples of excellence for all to witness. When criticized by others, offer continual examples of excellence as your only response.

Recognizing Achievements

Serve enthusiastically as a spokesperson for the accomplishments and concerns of others. Attentive leaders crusade for the issues, ideas, and achievements of those less able to speak for themselves giving ample recognition for their origin.

In the clashes between ignorance and intelligence, ignorance is generally the aggressor.
Paul Harris

The last of human freedoms—the ability to choose one's attitude in a given set of circumstances.
Viktor E. Frankl

Men of genius are admired; men of wealth are envied; men of power are feared; but only men of character are trusted.
Alfred Adler

How do such inspiring values of peace come from trained combatants of war? How were these peaceful values practiced by so many of the Tuskegee Airmen originating from all over the United States? They were really warriors of peace using compassion and excellence as their weapons of choice.

Instincts are powerful influences frequently encouraging our desires and actions to show jealousy, revenge, violence, aggression, greed, and other unfavorable behaviors. For me to override my instinctual desires, I must use a value system guided by intentional free choice. I am going to give you examples of heroes of peace and how they intentionally overcame their instincts of aggression replacing them with leadership, guidance, understanding, kindness, and generosity. Their stories are remarkable; their stories are true. We all have free choice at our beckoned call.

We can choose when to make love, when to nurture, and when to give to others. We decide if we should come to another's aide or walk the other way. It is entirely up to us if we build or destroy, if we inspire or discourage. We can voluntarily inflict pain or bring comfort; we can decide whether we use ethics and values or utilize greed and ruthlessness. Do you wish to guide and nurture children or scorn them into withdrawal? Is it your wish to respect and admire others or to control, put down, and embarrass them? Do you humiliate subordinates with harsh sarcasm or encourage their growth with suggestions and wisdom? Do you watch television or read books? Do you gamble or save? Our choices are endless, and we are faced with choices every second of every day. Seat belts? Smoking? That extra drink? Another five or ten miles per hour? My spouse will never find out. The chance of the IRS auditing me is very remote. My job is good enough. A graduation diploma is just a piece of paper. A marriage license is just a piece of paper. A peace treaty is just a piece of paper. No one is watching me; no one will know.

The first three of my selected twenty-five heroes to be discussed in this book are Nelson Mandela, Paul Harris, and Principal Peter Daniels. As you read the excerpts of each hero, try to see how their behavior and accomplishments fit the fourteen heroic values used throughout this book. This will give you insight into why I selected these individual heroes of peace. It would also be beneficial to compare the heroes' accomplishments to those of the Tuskegee Airmen, thus linking together the deeds, values, and methodologies of them all.

NELSON MANDELA
My Greatest Hero of Peace

Date of birth and death: July 18, 1918, to December 5, 2013
Profession: Politician, educator
Country: South Africa
Compassionate endeavor: Human rights, human equality
Nobel Prize—1993

Recognize your value, not just as God's creation, but as His masterpiece and
don't part with your dignity for any price or under any pressure.
Nelson Mandela

Out of all the heroes I have studied, Nelson Mandela is at the top of the list regarding his humanitarian endeavors, personal sacrifices, endurance, and practicing his pure values for the benefit and recognition of mankind.

The country of South Africa, after 1948, was governed by whites stemming from a secret all male society referred to as the Afrikaner Brotherhood. It was started in 1920 by Dutch whites desiring to promote their own interests and it was described as a "dangerous, cunning, political fascist organization."[68] Each South African prime minister and president from the beginning of Apartheid in 1948 to the end of Apartheid in 1994 was a member of the brotherhood.[69] "Apartheid" means "apartness" in the Afrikaans language.[70] Many believe the Apartheid government was the most oppressive second only to Nazi Germany. It came into power after the minority white population won the elections bringing the National Party, consisting of many Afrikaner Brotherhood members, into power.[71] At the time, 79% of the population in South Africa was black. The remaining white 21% of the population was, indeed, a minority.

Nelson Mandela was born on July 18, 1918, in the South African Village of Mevzo. His father was chief of the Thembu tribe. One of his father's cows escaped through a broken fence and caused damage to an-

---

68 Afrikaner Broederbon, Wikipedia
69 *TIME*, 2013, Special Commemorative Edition, Kelly Knauer, *Nelson Mandela, A Hero's Journey 1918-2013*, Time Home Entertainment, 135 West 50th St New York, NY 10020
70 History World, *History of South Africa, History of South Africa Timeline*, Gascoigne, Bamber. HistoryWorld. From 2001, ongoing. http://www.historyworld.net. Afrikaner Broederbond, From Wikipedia, https://en.wikipedia.org/wiki/Afrikaner_Broederbond
71 *Apartheid in South Africa, How the apartheid society was created*, http://www.rebirth.co.za/apartheid_history1.htm

other's property. Because of this negligence and a bad attitude with the white magistrate, Mandela's father was stripped of his chief position losing most of his land, cattle, and income. Despite this disgrace on his father, Mandela's heritage was from a line of chiefs, and he benefited from his lineage as he grew by receiving several considerations and opportunities.

Mandela's father died in 1927. Mandela was nine-years old at the time, two years after he started primary school. He was the first member of his family to receive a formal education. A few days after his father's funeral, Mandela went to live with Chief Jongintaba, a friend of Mandela's father, who adopted Mandela a short time later.[72]

Education is the most powerful weapon which you can use to change the world.
Nelson Mandela

Mandela grew up fighting for the rights of all people. His greatness, sacrifices, wisdom, and courage helped him maintain his dignity through-out his trials fighting the Apartheid government and to eventually become the first black and democratically elected president of South Africa.

Nelson Mandela arrested

On July 11, 1963, Nelson Mandela and nine other members of the A.N.C. (African National Congress), were arrested on a privately-owned farm in Rivonia, a suburb of Johannesburg, and charged with conspiracy to overthrow the Apartheid government. Their trial, known as the Rivonia Trial, lasted nine months. On June 12, 1964, at trial's end, Nelson Mandela and seven other members of his A.N.C., having been found guilty, were sentenced to confinement for life in prison. Mandela and six other black cohorts were sent to Robben Island prison, about 8 miles offshore from Cape Town, South Africa.[73] One Caucasian defendant was sent to a prison for whites. Two of the ten defendants were found not guilty.

Nelson Mandela's life in Robben Island Prison

At Robben Island Prison, Mandela was permitted to write and receive one, 500-word, highly censored letter every six months, but only to or from an

---

72 *Mandela, The Authorized Portrait,* Andrews McMeel Publishing LLC, in association with PQ Blackwell
73 Ibid

immediate family member—no one else.[74] These and other restrictive rules fluctuated throughout the years as management changed and prisoners earned more privileges.

For almost the first year on Robben Island, Nelson Mandela was smashing big rocks into gravel with a hammer in the main courtyard. There were two rows of ten prisoners doing this same task, and no one could talk to one another. In January of 1965, Mandela and his Rivonia Trial cronies were transferred to the island's limestone quarry. Mandela and his fellow prisoners were promised they would only be assigned to the limestone quarry for six months. After thirteen years, they were still waiting for their reassignment out of the quarry's blazing summer heat and freezing winter conditions. After his first three years in the quarry, Mandela's tear ducts were permanently sealed from the limestone dust preventing him from crying.[75]

Mandela stated, "the authorities never explained why we had been taken from the courtyard to the quarry. It was an attempt to crush our spirits. But those first few weeks at the quarry had the opposite effect on us. Despite blistered and bleeding hands, we were invigorated."[76]

Nelson Mandela wrote in his autobiography, "Prison and the authorities conspire to rob each man of his dignity. In and of itself, that assured that I would survive, for any man or institution that tries to rob me of my dignity will lose because I will not part with it at any price or under any pressure."

The limestone quarry offered advantages over the courtyard, however, and one of the biggest advantages was that the prisoners could talk to each other—and talk they did as will become most evident in the next few paragraphs.

---

74 Ibid *Letters from Robben Island, A selection of Ahmed Kathrada's prison correspondence, 1964-1989*, Zebra Press, PO Box 1144, Cape Town, South Africa, Michigan State University Press 1999
75 TIME, 2013, Special Commemorative Edition, Kelly Knauer, Nelson Mandela, *A Hero's Journey 1918-2013*, Time Home Entertainment, 135 West 50th St New York, NY 10020
76 *Long Walk to Freedom*, by Nelson Mandela, Abridged Edition, 1994, Little Brown and Co. Ltd., London, UK

In 2004, I photographed the cave on the far wall of the quarry depicted in this photograph. When any of the prisoners had to relieve themselves, they dug a hole in the cave floor, did their business, and then buried it. It wasn't too long before they started digging up another's prior burial. There was no more room on the cave floor for new holes. The guards would not allow digging outside the cave because of future limestone harvests.[77]

Who was imprisoned at Robben Island?

When oppressive governments fill their jails with dissidents, such prisoners are frequently comprised of two main types: (1) The uneducated soldiers and rebels of the opposing side, and (2) the highly educated nonconformists (doctors, lawyers, political leaders) that could organize rebellions against the government if they were free to do so. Therefore, in such circumstances, the prisoners were comprised of the unschooled and the highly educated. Or as Nelson Mandela looked at it, the professors and the students.[78]

It wasn't long before the prison was known as Robben Island University. Educated prisoners were lecturing on their areas of expertise whether it be the United States Constitution, Karl Marx, homosexuality, English, mathematics, or the history of South Africa and its various tribal rivalries. When new prisoners arrived at Robben Island, mostly consisting of young political dissidents rebelling against the Apartheid government, they proudly announced to their family and friends that they were on their way to "Mandela University!"[79]

There were no classrooms

These lectures were not held in formal classrooms, for there were none,

77 Told to the author at Robben Island, July 2004, by a tour guide at Robben Island Prison who had been a prisoner with Nelson Mandela
78 Ibid
79 *TIME*, 2013, Special Commemorative Edition, Kelly Knauer, *Nelson Mandela, A Hero's Journey 1918-2013*, Time Home Entertainment, 135 West 50th St New York, NY 10020

but rather in social circles as prisoners dug for limestone in the quarry. Prison guards often tried to break up these circles of learning by ordering the prisoners to do more digging for limestone, but eventually even some of the guards decided to listen to the lectures. Often healthy debates on various subjects were taking place within these learning-circles interrupted occasionally by shovels digging for limestone for a minute or two acting as a front for working. When the guards were not in the mood to tolerate the learning circles in the quarry, the prisoners would then form smaller clusters of two or three men to discuss their lessons. During lunch breaks, they would gather in larger groups in the shed used for meals and covered more academic ground.[80]

Nelson Mandela wrote "Robben Island was known as the University. This is not only because of what we learned from books, or because prisoners studied English, Afrikaans, art, geography, and mathematics, or because so many of our men…earned multiple degrees. Robben Island was known as the University because of what we learned from each other. We became our own faculty, with our own professors, our own curriculum, our own courses…Teaching conditions were not ideal. Study groups would work together in the quarry and station themselves in a circle around the leader of the seminar. The style of teaching was Socratic in nature; ideas and theories were elucidated through leaders asking and answering questions." [81]

There can be no greater gift than that of giving one's time and energy to help others without expecting anything in return.
Nelson Mandela

What are "Socratic in nature" teaching methods?

Socrates was a Greek philosopher and is considered by many as the father of western philosophy (469-399 BCE). His primary student was Plato who became the principal instructor for Aristotle. To continue the chain of knowledge, Aristotle conveyed Socrates' teaching methods to Alexander the Great who spread them throughout Asia Minor, Egypt, and Mesopotamia to India.

---

80 Brand South Africa (Official Custodian of South Africa's Nation Brand), SAinfo Reporter, July 10, 2013, Mandela's Robben Island University
81 *Long Walk to Freedom*, by Nelson Mandela, Abridged Edition, 1994, Little Brown and Co. Ltd., London, UK

Socrates's teaching methodology involved debating a series of questions presented after a lecture to stimulate critical thinking and used these inquiries as tests of logic and fact. Students did not take notes. There were no written exams. There was no rote memorization. There was no lesson plan. Students learned from repeated interactions among the group trying to draw logical conclusions by debating the verbally presented material. Both the leader and students asked probing questions trying to explore the many facets of each debated subject. Each student prisoner was given an assignment which included leading a seminar for the other students. At that time, they would be in the center of the learning circle conveying their wisdom to others coupled with a series of questions to be debated.[82]

Because of the frequent secret nature for lessons taught at Robben Island University, Socratic teaching methods were often necessary to prevent discovery. A deep passion for learning and acquired knowledge coupled with a pursuit for wisdom replaced the need for a standardized curriculum.

Maintaining one's dignity at Robben Island

Guarding his priceless dignity from all disruptive occurrences and maintaining a strong vision of an optimistic future was a paramount and primary goal for Nelson Mandela. Sustaining these values allowed him to survive under the horrible conditions he experienced while being in prison for twenty-seven years.

Mandela once said, "I had read some of the classic Greek plays in prison and found them enormously elevating. What I took out of them was that character was measured by facing up to difficult situations and that a hero was a man who would not break even under the most trying circumstances."[83]

Secret ways of communicating

Mandela, through great persistence, was eventually able to acquire the great books of literature, history, politics, and philosophy from the Red Cross. These books greatly aided in the prisoners' studies. The prison guards, however, often refused to allow the books to be exchanged between inmates and frequently issued book restrictions and the suspension-of-study-time

---

82 *Stanford University Newsletter on Teaching*, fall 2003, Vol 13, No. 1, The Socratic Method: What it is and How to Use it in the Classroom
83 *Training Leaders of Leaders*, Andrea S. N. Brown, andrea@andreabrown.org, Robben Island: The University sentenced to prison December 9, 2013

as a punishment for rule infractions. At one time the Robben Island Prison administration encouraged the prisoners to take correspondence courses to improve themselves; at other times there was severe punishment for studying and possessing books. Secret ways of communicating with other prisoners had to be in place as rules changed.[84]

Sometimes prisoners created false bottoms in match boxes. Hidden messages were inserted under the false bottom and the match boxes were dropped at strategic locations by prisoners walking to work at the quarry. Later, other prisoners would retrieve the match boxes and read the secret messages.

Other ways of writing secret notes was to write them with milk instead of ink. The white milk writing could not be seen on white paper, but when sprayed with the disinfectant used to clean the cells, the writing became visible.[85]

Making your own chess pieces

If you can find a piece of paper and a pen, you can play chess. I took this photograph of pen-drawn chess pieces at Robben Island in 2004. They are the actual paper pieces used by Mandela and other prisoners.

Mandela University

Although Mandela was sentenced to prison for life, he spent twenty-seven years in confinement before he was released. Eighteen of those twenty-seven years were spent at Robben Island.

Mandela studied law through a correspondence school at London University[86] and often represented his fellow prisoners in appeal cases at Robben Island. Various correspondence schools serving other prisoners soon joined the Robben Island education family and took advantage of the "University" being filled with professors and curricula.[87]

84 *Long Walk to Freedom,* by Nelson Mandela, Abridged Edition, 1994, Little Brown and Co. Ltd., London, UK
85 Ibid
86 *TIME,* 2013, Special Commemorative Edition, Kelly Knauer, *Nelson Mandela, A Hero's Journey 1918-2013,* Time Home Entertainment, 135 West 50th St New York, NY 10020
87 *Long Walk to Freedom,* by Nelson Mandela, Abridged Edition, 1994, Little Brown and Co. Ltd., London, UK

Mandela started an "underground" political studies track to prepare some educationally-advanced prisoners for the upcoming political arenas in South Africa should they eventually be released.[88] These political studies, as well as studies in military history, were not allowed at Robben Island, nor by the Apartheid government; therefore, the aforementioned secret ways of communicating among the inmate students had to be utilized.

There is no passion to be found in playing small—in settling for a life that is less than you are capable of living.
Nelson Mandela

What would you do if sentenced to life in prison?

Would you not become severely depressed if you were sentenced to life in a prison whose guards and supervisors were inhumane, in a prison where you crushed big rocks into gravel with a hammer for 10-hours a day? What if your jail cell was only 8 feet x 6 feet, no bed (only a grass mat), and no toilet (only a metal bucket)? Ah, but let's not forget the gourmet meals: maize (corn) porridge and maize-based coffee for breakfast, boiled maize for lunch, and dinner was more maize and a small vegetable[89] Do you imagine you would lose your ambition in such a place, your lust for life, your motivation, desire, and especially your self-esteem and dignity?

The old expression, "When life hands you a lemon, make lemonade," applies to Nelson Mandela. After being sentenced to life in prison, an inhumane prison with cruel guards exercising brutality and humiliation, Mandela never lost his dignity, and never gave up hope of an eventual release. In the interim, he created a university and educated hundreds of inmates with many receiving multiple college degrees. The multitude of obstacles Mandela had to overcome to make Robben Island University a reality was almost insurmountable. Mandela's dedication to his students and university could arguably be unparalleled. He was an incredible hero of peace for himself first, and then for others.

---

88 Prism Decision Systems, Sean Brady, December 6, 2013, Nelson Mandela's inspiring limestone quarry classroom https://www.prismdecision.com/nelson-mandelas-inspiring-limestone-quarry-classroom/
89 *TIME*, 2013, Special Commemorative Edition, Kelly Knauer, Nelson Mandela, A Hero's Journey 1918-2013, Time Home Entertainment, 135 West 50th St New York, NY 10020

*After climbing a great hill, one only finds that there are
many more hills to climb.*
Nelson Mandela

Nelson Mandela saw the value of every person regardless of stature
Nelson Mandela believed in equality of all humans. He believed a person's importance is not based on their position, title, wealth. or otherwise. All people are equally valued. As an example, the president of the United States might jeopardize his reputation and dignity if he wore mud-covered shoes to an important black-tie meeting with world dignitaries. This means the shoe-shine man working for the president is important. The shoe-shine man is partially responsible for the quality of the president's reputation. All people everywhere, in one way or another, hold similar responsibilities.

To further illustrate this, after Nelson Mandela was elected the president of South Africa, a CEO from an American company made an appointment to meet Mandela at his home. Doing business in South Africa without encountering the uncertainty of the former Apartheid government was the topic to be discussed. At the designated time for the meeting, a black limousine drove into Mandela's driveway. The CEO's chauffeur got out of the limousine and walked around to open the rear door for the CEO. Mandela, seeing the limo enter his driveway, appeared at the front door of the house as the CEO left the limo and walked toward Mandela. Friendly greetings were shared. The limo driver stood by the car as the CEO and Mandela entered the home.

Once inside, Mandela and the CEO took their seats at a table. A few other niceties were exchanged, and then Mandela sat still without talking for several minutes. Mandela looked out the window, looked around the room, glanced at the CEO and smiled, and remained silent. The CEO sensed something was out of the ordinary and asked Mandela, "Sir, are we waiting for someone else?"

Mandela answered, "Yes, I am waiting for your man in the driveway."

The CEO replied, "Oh, he's just the chauffeur. There is no reason he should join us."

With that, Mandela got up from the table and went out to the driveway. The chauffeur was still standing by the limo. Mandela invited him to come into the house and join the meeting, which he did.

The meeting lasted about one hour with the chauffeur sitting at the table the entire time. When the meeting was over, the CEO and the chauffeur exchanged pleasantries with Mandela, returned to the limo, and drove away. Shortly after they had entered the main highway, the chauffeur addressed the CEO by saying, "Thank you, sir, for asking Mandela to come outside and invite me to your meeting."

The CEO replied, "You're welcome."

Don't lose faith in the integrity of this American CEO, for initially his behavior reflected poor values, but he felt so bad about what he told the chauffeur, that a few days later he called the chauffeur into his office and confessed the entire incident.[90]

And as we let our own light shine, we unconsciously give other people permission to do the same.
Nelson Mandela

Don't judge me by my successes; judge me by how many times I fell down and got back up again.
Nelson Mandela

---

90 Nelson Mandela autobiography

PAUL HARRIS
Created the World's Largest Society of Compassion
Rotary Assisted
Profession: Businessman, founder of Rotary International
Country: U.S.A. and then the world
Compassionate endeavor: Rotary International

What is Rotary International?

As of 2020, Rotary International consists of local community volunteers all around the world working together to help fight disease; promote peace; provide clean water, sanitation, and hygiene; save mothers and children; support education; and grow local economies. Members consist of everyday people like businessmen and women, school teachers, medical personnel, construction workers, farmers, government employees, etc.

How did Rotary International get started by Paul Harris?

On February 23, 1905, Paul Harris, a lawyer practicing in Chicago, called three of his friends to a meeting in his office. The purpose of the meeting was to start an organization that could offer advice and fellowship for new businessmen in the area. This was the first Rotary club meeting. Shortly the purpose of Rotary meetings expanded to include community service and humanitarian projects. The term "Rotary" was established because the meeting locations originally rotated between members.

Harris wanted to start many new clubs. The second Rotary Club was founded in San Francisco in 1908. By 1910, fifteen new clubs had started in major cities across the United States. That August, the existing 16 Rotary Clubs held their first national convention in Chicago.

Paul Harris died in 1947 at age 78; he was committed to the humanitarian concept of Rotary for forty-two years. At the time of his death, over 6,000 Rotary Clubs existed in 75 countries with 200,000 members and has currently expanded (2020) to over 35,000 Rotary Clubs in over 200 countries and territories comprised of 1.2 million members.[91] On the average since 1905 through 2019, 299 new Rotary Clubs were formed throughout the world each year with 10,256 new members joining annually.[92]

---

91 Rotary International, www.rotary.com
92 Ibid

A humanitarian organization beyond comprehension

It is one thing to start an organization that grows to a giant corporation. United Airlines, Apple Computer, and the American Red Cross might be such examples. It is quite another thing to create an organization that accomplishes humanitarian tasks beyond the comprehension of the human brain. You are about to see why Paul Harris is listed among my chosen heroes of peace.

In 1979, Rotary International decided to eradicate polio throughout the world.[93] Polio is a paralyzing and often deadly disease usually affecting children under the age of five. The spread of the polio virus usually occurs from drinking contaminated water. The virus attacks the human nervous system causing victims to become crippled. The resulting limb contortions are often grotesque.

In 1955, an effective polio vaccine was developed by Dr. Jonas Salk in Cape Town, South Africa. Although there is no cure for those already suffering from polio, Salk's vaccine, consisting of two drops of a liquid into the mouth of a child, will prevent the disease from occurring in those not yet exposed. But how could the world's children be immunized?

Rotary International started their PolioPlus program in 1985. This was the largest internationally coordinated program for a massive effort to aide public health anywhere on our globe. Volunteers and donations came from Rotary Clubs around the world, from the World Health Organization (WHO), and from the Bill and Melinda Gates foundation. By 1994, Polio was eliminated from North and South America.

Beyond the mind's comprehension

After it was believed that polio had been eliminated in India, one new case was reported in 1995. This resulted in an unbelievable massive organization

---

93 Ibid

consisting of Rotary, WHO, United Nations Children's' Fund (UNICEF), U.S. Centers for Disease Control and Prevention (CDC) and Indian government volunteers. Over one million coordinated volunteers arrived and met in various Indian locations and established 640,000 vaccination booths. Because the polio vaccine had to be kept refrigerated, 200 million doses of the polio vaccines were carried by volunteers wrapped in six million ice packs and delivered to 190 million homes.[94] Volunteers utilized cars, trucks, horses, canoes, elephants, camels, and even walked on foot to arrive at the most remote Indian villages. In one day, 125 million Indian children five years of age or younger were inoculated against polio. That equals to 86,805 immunizations every minute; that's 1,447 children inoculated every second! I would have not thought this was possible! Paul Harris, the seeds of your Rotary International organization have grown beyond belief!

Rotary volunteers continue to fight polio

In 2006, new cases of polio had dropped from 122 countries to only four: Afghanistan, Pakistan, Nigeria, and India.[95] As of 2019, Rotary International has helped to immunize 2.5 billion children located in 122 countries. Polio has been reduced 99.9 % throughout the world because of these gargantuan efforts. Rotary International volunteers continued to try and stop the remaining .1% of polio outbreaks. War, political unrest restricting inoculations in certain areas, and hard-to-reach villages requiring canoes to access, continued to serve as obstacles to volunteers.[96] One factor that has caused a great problem in the eradication of polio is the airplane, regularly transporting polio carriers to other countries.

Whatever Rotary means to us, to the world it will be judged
by the results it achieves.
Paul Harris

The less one knows, the more he thinks he knows, and the more willing he is to
employ any and all measures to enforce his views upon others.
Paul Harris

When Rotarians volunteer to immunize children against polio, they go on a NID (National Immunization Days) trip to the country in need. Rotarians cover their own expenses for food, transportation, lodging and everything else. Many children needing polio immunizations are in poor, underdeveloped countries, and many of these locations are experiencing

---

94 The Source The-Source.net
95 *Polio Global Irradiation Initiative*, http://polioeradication.org/polio-today/history-of-polio/
96 Ibid

armed conflict and war. How do Rotarian volunteers vaccinate children against polio in the middle of an active battlefield?

Members of Rotary International met with agents from WHO, UNICEF, and the Inter-Agency Standing Committee (IASC)[97] to coordinate cease-fire events between protagonists, rebel armies, militias, and government troops allowing the inoculation of children against polio. These arranged cease-fire events among the opposing sides of armed conflicts are called Days of Tranquility.

I personally think such a massive undertaking would be almost impossible, especially among rebel armies and insurgents determined to expeditiously eliminate their enemies. How could the leaders of these forces be contacted? How could safe meeting places be determined? Were these lay-down-your-arms negotiations ever successful? Did fighting really stop so children could be immunized against polio? When I was given these statistics from Rotary International, I did not believe what I was reading! Here are only a few of the many successful cease-fire negotiations:

- March 13-19, 2001—the Taliban and the Northern Alliance— Afghanistan; 1999, three million children immunized.
- Angola; 1994, Corridors of Peace established with NATO's help.
- Bosnia; June 11, 2000, 11 million children immunized.
- Democratic Republic of Congo; 1999, 250,000 children immunized.
- El Salvador; 1987 Corridors of Peace established for vaccines.
- Lebanon; November 10, 2000, 30-day cease fire for unimpeded movement of humanitarian workers.
- Sierra Leone; September—October 1999, Corridors of Peace established.
- Other countries where cease-fire negotiations were successfully negotiated so children could be vaccinated were Tajikistan, Sudan, Santo Domingo, Philippines, Iraq, Sri Lanka, and Uganda.

As of 2018-2019, Rotary International volunteers worked 47 million hours per year. There were 1,189,466 Rotarians in 35,890 Rotary Clubs volunteering this work. In 2019, Rotarians furnished $850,000,000 worth of community service projects, created $97,894,871 of grants for the needy, and created $9.00 of social and economic problem-solving efforts for every $1.00 it cost Rotary to produce.[98]

---

97 The Inter-Agency Standing Committee (ISAC) is the main forum for major humanitarian agencies to ensure inter-agency decision-making in response to complex emergencies, including needs assessment, consolidated appeals, and field coordination arrangements.
98 Rotary International, The Rotary Foundation, Annual Report 2018-2019

To attempt to superimpose its views through the exercise of force, is seldom the part of intelligence; it is frequently the part of ignorance.

Paul Harris

Of the twenty-five heroes of peace discussed in this book, thirteen of them have been assisted by Rotary clubs as they accomplished their heroic endeavors. They are marked in the table of contents.

PRINCIPAL PETER DANIELS
Turns Criminals into Angels—Rotary Assisted
Profession: Primary School Principal
Country: Paarl, South Africa
Compassionate endeavor: Child values and education

Around the year 2000 in a small town called Paarl, South Africa, there was an elementary school for grades K-7. It consisted only of male students, for females were thought unable to acquire as much knowledge as males and would not sufficiently contribute to supplement the future economy.

Crime interfered with education
The Nederburg Primary School was situated in the middle of the turf connecting six-territorial gangs. Frequent gang fights erupted around the school as gangs fought each other for territory and the entrapment of the school children for drugs and prostitution.

The new principal was Peter Daniels. He was an ambitious, kind, and gentle man, one of my primary heroes. I am not sure he knew what was in store for him when he accepted his new position as principal. His first day on the job, he found it necessary to develop a plan for his students to hide on the floor under their desks as bullets frequently zinged through the classrooms. The second day he started a project to repair over 800 bullet holes throughout the school. He quickly learned about the six-rival gangs having their turf wars on the school property. His next move was to call an investigative meeting with the leaders of all six gangs. He was taking his

life in his hands, but this was certainly a new approach for the gang leaders, so they attended the meeting mostly out of curiosity, but they had to first declare a truce so no one would be shot at the gathering.

The meeting of gang leaders proved to be beneficial

At this summit of gang leaders, Principal Daniels asked "why" shooting wars were necessary, especially on the school property? Daniels was informed by Danny, one of top the gang leaders, that the unemployment in the area was 70%, that few of the gang members could find any jobs, that the gangs have been fighting each other for over forty years, and that if they do not commit crimes (robbing, stealing, etc.), they cannot feed their families. It was just an accepted way of life.

Principal Daniels knew there was a large area of land on school property (a few acres) intended for athletic fields should enough money be raised in the future. Principal Daniels proposed to the six-gang leaders: "There is a large plot of land at the Nederburg Primary School that I am willing to allow your gangs to use for raising fruits and vegetables. You could then sell these crops at a roadside stand and hopefully raise enough money to support your families. You would no longer need to steal. There are some conditions, however, and we need to agree on them."

- The shooting wars must stop, at least on school property.
- Your six gangs must declare a truce and work together planting and harvesting the crops.
- The small farm will be called "The Peace Garden."
- You may sell the crops by erecting curbside stands on the Nederburg Primary School property.

- Your six gangs must work together selling the crops and fairly distribute the revenue.
- If you have any crops left over that you cannot sell, this produce must be donated to the children of Nederburg Primary School, the local old-aged home, or the local hospital.

Principal Daniels wanted to trust the gangsters to comply with his plan and all the terms of the agreement. Could he trust the gangsters? The safety of the school children was a stake!

Trusting only the trustworthy is not trusting at all.
Carol Ruggie

The gang leaders held a huddled conference and agreed to the terms and conditions, but other problems had to be resolved. Where were the seeds going to be obtained? Where was the necessary water going to originate? How would any water obtained be applied to the land?

The entire community was to benefit
Principal Daniels's creative proposal quickly spread about the community because it benefited so many people. By finding income for the gangsters, the crime rate should be greatly reduced benefiting the entire area. From the gangsters earning their own spending money, local merchants would benefit from increased sales. One fear was that local grocery stores would have their produce sales decreased as the gangsters sold their crops to the public. As it turned out, because there were no harassing gangsters hanging around local stores, citizens were no longer afraid to shop, and the sales of local merchants actually increased.

Other organizations hearing of this creative plan offered support. The local Department of Agricultural generously provided a sprinkler system for the land. The Mayor of Paarl offered to supply city water for the Peace Garden if the gangsters swept some of the city streets at night.

The Peace Garden came into being
The Peace Garden came to fruition in 2003. Not one shot was fired the entire year nor were there any burglaries at the school. The gangsters were successful in planting crops, in declaring a peace among the gangs, in supporting their families from the sale of fruits and vegetables, and in

supplying surplus crops to Nederburg Primary School, the old-age home, and the local hospital.

Crime was unnoticeable. The children at the Nederburg Primary School were safe. Principal Daniels received wonderful media publicity throughout all South Africa.

My co-researcher, Carol Ruggie, to encourage girl's acceptance and attendance at the school, started a scholarship for girls at Nederburg Primary School. But first, she flew Principal Daniels from South Africa to her home in Aurora, Ohio, so Daniels could see how girls in the Aurora School System were not only keeping pace with the boys, but frequently surpassing them. Principal Daniels, after seeing the intelligence and ability of primary-school girls, was amazed and convinced of the equality between the genders. He returned to Nederburg Primary School and encouraged girls to enroll equally with boys.[99]

I visited Principal Daniels

In 2004, I visited Principal Daniels at his school. I noticed there seemed to be as many girls as boys in every classroom. Principal Daniels invited me to meet hundreds of his students at an outside assembly on the school's courtyard. Before the meeting officially started, all the students started praying. I commented to my assigned interpreter, "It is nice that meetings are started with a prayer. It is like our Rotary Club meeting back in the states. We pray before every meeting."

My interpreter stated that I was incorrect. She sadly informed me, "They are praying for their family members and classmates that died or were killed during the prior week!" My heart sank into remorseful silence.

After my wonderful meeting with the children, Principal Daniels informed me that the leaders of the six gangs were assembled and eager to meet with me. He said they were waiting for me at the Peace Garden. I was extremely excited. [100]

I met the gangster leaders

I walked out to the Peace Garden to find eight men waiting for me. I was warmly welcomed by them all. They showed me the Peace Garden, their many growing fruits and vegetables, the sprinkler system, and the stand where they sell their vegetables. They were proud and happy that

---

99 From a one-day interview with Principal Peter Daniels, a tour of his school, an interview with the six-gang leaders, and constant feedback from Carol Ruggie, founder of the Nederburg Primary Scholarship for girls.
100 Ibid

they could support themselves and their families while helping the entire community.

The gang leaders then thanked me and posed for a photograph (right). I was curious why they were thanking me, for I had done nothing to contribute to their marvelous accomplishments. I was informed that Principal Daniels implied that I was coming to see them from Ohio, USA, to offer my knowledge and advice in helping them be successful. They told me they were grateful to me for such a major undertaking designed to benefit them. They then said they were ready to listen to my advice. I apologized for any misunderstanding about my visit, but that I was writing a book about heroes of peace around the world, and I considered them all heroes. I had come to South Africa from Ohio to interview them, to learn from their great accomplishments, and to take home with me their knowledge and advice to benefit the American people. I had not come to South Africa to teach them, but to learn from them and then share their remarkable ways. That was a priceless moment for me.

They were filled with disbelief

They all looked at me in total silence. They could not believe what I just said. They never considered themselves heroes or knowledgeable enough to help Americans. I assured them their accomplishments were most remarkable and will serve as a sterling example for the rest of the world. It was my intention, through my book about heroes of peace, to promote their magnificence for everyone to study, to copy, and to admire. I then thanked them in great admiration for meeting me.

I interviewed them about their families, how they liked working together peacefully, how they felt about helping the children at the Nederburg Primary school, whether they thought they would ever return to crime, and what values they considered necessary to hold dear to continue their new way of life?

Danny was on parole for manslaughter, and a criminal record of violence was not foreign to any of them. I wanted to know how they transformed from violent criminals to loving, ambitious, and productive community members? My interviews with them were most inspiring.

Gang members in the Peace Garden

Closing Thoughts

If you maintain the dignity of your enemies, you will defeat them faster and with fewer casualties. If you maintain the dignity of your employees, you will train them faster, and receive more quality output. They will be more productive, be true ambassadors for your firm, and result in less turnover. If you maintain the dignity of your children, they will grow strong, believe in themselves, reach their goals, have ambition, and often experience success sooner. If you always maintain your dignity, you will experience great inner peace and automatically respect others as you do yourself.

Being constantly in the public eye gives me a special responsibility, to sensitize the world to an important cause, to defend certain values.
Diana, Princess of Wales

An optimist is a person who sees a green light everywhere, while a pessimist sees only the red stoplight. . . The truly wise person is color-blind.
Albert Schweitzer

If you judge people, you have no time to love them.
Mother Teresa

Chapter Three
The Values of Developing Vision and Overcoming Obstacles

Developing Vision
Envision things as wonderful as they can be, not as they are, and then strive to create positive change toward these envisioned goals. All great accomplishments started as a vision that others could not see.

Overcoming Obstacles
Realize that obstacles are not barriers to your goals, but opportunities for growth and challenges to enrich your self-confidence by mastering new skills. A person having reached a goal without overcoming obstacles has learned nothing and accomplished even less. Conquered obstacles are the only qualifying credentials of heroes and a measure of your commitment and leadership.

If you can sit quietly after difficult news, if in financial downturns you remain perfectly calm, if you can see your neighbors travel to fantastic places without a twinge of jealously, if you can happily eat whatever is put on your plate and fall asleep after a day of running around without a drink or pill, if you can always find contentment just where you are, then you are probably a dog.
Jack Kornfield

Whoever undertakes to set himself up as judge in the field of truth and knowledge is shipwrecked by the laughter of the Gods.
Albert Einstein

Your heart has eyes that your brain knows nothing about.
Unknown

Children often do not realize their limitations; therefore, many of them think they do not have any. When their hearts are also filled with the unconditional love of Mother Teresa, the determination of Booker T. Washington, and the optimism of Gandhi, you often have an unfolding story of success and inspiration.

Occasionally, these children grow into adults while maintaining their rare optimism and positive outlook. From these individuals, when in a crisis, our future heroes of peace are often born.

Investigating the true heroes of peace was one of the most rewarding aspects of my research. I expected to be impressed with the accomplishments of great heroes like Nelson Mandela, Eleanor Roosevelt, and Albert Schweitzer. But when I started studying the remarkable accomplishments of impoverished people in third-world countries, especially some children, I was truly blown away. What happens when a ten-year-old girl in Canada follows the passion, values, and discipline employed by Desmond Tutu? What can be accomplished when an eleven-year-old boy in Africa uses the persistence and enthusiasm of Dr. Martin Luther King in perusing his humanitarian visions? A six-year-old boy in Canada tries to help some African children; fifteen years later he has installed over 360 water wells in several third-world countries. How many starving families can be fed when a man living in a shack in an African township places the values and determination of my selected heroes into his tiny entrepreneurial project?

Eventually I asked myself, "If these wonderful children with limited education, recourses, and connections can accomplish so many extraordinary undertakings, why can't anyone who wants to do so?" They can.

My Heroes of Peace discussed in this chapter— Hannah Taylor, Ryan Hreljac, and Efran Penaflorida—show how it's done.

HANNAH TAYLOR
A Child Caring for the Homeless—Rotary Assisted
Profession: Student (at the time of this narrative)
Country: Winnipeg, Canada
Compassionate endeavor: Serving the homeless

When Hannah Taylor was five years old, her mother drove her to a shopping center. It was a freezing day in winter. There she saw a homeless man looking for food in a garbage can. Hannah did not understand why people had to be hungry or homeless. She excitedly asked her mother to stop the car! Hannah then left the car and ran to the homeless man. Hannah immediately reached into her little purse and gave the homeless man all her money—a few nickels, some pennies, a lint ball, and a small toy ladybug. She then ran back to her mom who was quite concerned. After a short-but-earnest lecture about not running up to strangers, Hannah and her mom entered the shopping mall.

The homeless man looked at the money Hannah gave him and found the toy ladybug. Thinking that Hannah did not mean to give him the ladybug, the homeless man spent several hours looking for Hannah and her mother. Finally, he located them as they were leaving the shopping mall. The homeless man returned to Hannah her ladybug.

Hannah became genuinely concerned about the homeless, for this sad situation was something new for her. She could not imagine going to sleep at night on a park bench or under a bridge or being hungry without any food and searching through garbage cans for something to eat!

Hannah asked her parents for some advice on how to raise money for the homeless. Her mom and dad started to think, and then thought about the homeless man returning the toy ladybug. By the age of eight years old, in May of 2004, Hannah started the Ladybug Foundation, a charitable organization dedicated to doing all it can to help put an end to homelessness. [101]

From seeing a homeless man go through garbage to speaking all over the world

Hannah started speaking in front of various groups trying to raise money to fight homelessness. Eventually she had presented programs at over 175 schools and in front of gatherings as large as 16,000 people. She has raised over $3 million just from the good people in Canada.[102]

The Ladybug Foundation Education Program Inc. is another charity that Hannah formed allowing her to address students in K-12 educational levels to "make a change" in the world by helping others. She has traveled throughout her native Canada speaking and spreading her message of hope and need to thousands of people. Hanna Taylor has made presentations to help the homeless all over the world. She has spoken throughout Canada, the United States, France, Sweden, and Singapore. Hannah's Ladybug

---

101 The Lady-Bug Foundation, Hannah Taylor, http://www.ladybugfoundation.ca/who-we-are/hannah-taylor-founder/
102 Ibid

Foundation has supported over fifty soup kitchens, emergency shelters, youth hostels, and missions designed to help the destitute. When she was thirteen years old, she was nationally listed as one of the most influential women in Canada.

National Red-Scarf Day is every January 31, another effort by Hannah to raised money for our homeless friends. By selling ladybug ornamented red scarfs and Ladybug T-shirts, Hannah increases the resources she has for helping others.

Hannah also hosts Big Bosses' lunches, where she meets with leaders of the business community and convinces them to help raise funds for the homeless. At one bosses' lunch, Hannah drew pictures of lady bugs on paper with crayons and auctioned them off to businessmen. The lowest bid price was $10,000.[103]

Hannah came to my rescue at a moment's notice

I called Hanna Taylor in April of 2010 to ask if she would come speak at my Rotary District Conference held in Beachwood, Ohio. She advised me she was presently in Amsterdam giving a talk and would be flying back to Winnipeg, Canada, her home, at the time of our Rotary Conference. She then said she would be happy to change her plane reservations from Amsterdam to Cleveland, Ohio, to Winnipeg, Canada. I was delighted. I was also extremely impressed with her spirit of service and compassion.

Hannah and her father attended the Rotary District Conference where Hannah was our dinner keynote speaker. She is a wonderful speaker, very captivating, and her compassion is transferred to others who listen. I placed fifty, black-spotted, ladybug banks on each table at the conference, and we collected over $1,000 for Hannah and her cause. Not as much as a businessman's luncheon, to be sure, but every little bit helps.

I thought if Hannah can do these compassionate endeavors starting at 5 years old, what could I have accomplish with my decades of experience? I felt inadequate.

---

103 I was told this by Hannah Taylor and her father at a Beachwood, Ohio, Rotary District Conference that Hannah Taylor was gracious enough to attend and speak in 2010. Hannah was fifteen years old at the time.

RYAN HRELJAC
A Canadian Child Caring for Poor Uganda Children—Rotary Assisted
Profession: Student (At the time of this narrative)
Country: Winnipeg, Canada
Compassionate endeavor: Water for the destitute

Ryan was six years old and in kindergarten when his teacher told his class about people in a village in Uganda, Africa. These villagers might die because their village has no water. The teacher suggested, to indoctrinate the kids into community service concepts, that the kindergarten class could raise $70 to help pay for a water well in this little village.

Ryan was excited at the thought of helping villagers in such terrible trouble. One misunderstanding was he thought the water well cost $70.00.

He went home and told his mother he wanted to earn $70 for a water well in Uganda. For months Ryan helped clean the house, rake leaves, wash the car, etc., until he earned $70.00.

Ryan was now in the 1st grade, took his $70 with his mother to his former kindergarten teacher. Ryan proudly held his hands, containing the $70, upward to the teacher. She said to Ryan, "Oh thank you, but water wells cost thousands of dollars!" Ryan became quiet. He slowly looked at his mother, and then turned and looked up at his former teacher. He was deep in thought. Finally, he said, "OK, I'll just have to work harder."

Ryan then gave talks to all the first-grade classes in his entire school district about the water crisis in the little African village. He encouraged hundreds of kids to work odd jobs at home to raise money for the water well in Uganda. "Ask your mom if you can earn money by raking leaves, pulling weeds, vacuuming the carpets, doing the dishes, etc.," Ryan pleaded. Within one year, Ryan, and hundreds of his hard-working friends, had collected enough money for the water well. They sent the money to the little village in Uganda where the well was successfully installed. The villagers named it "Ryan's Well."

Ryan was communicating with the villagers through email and developed a friendship with a boy named Jimmy. Ryan was told by Jimmy how wonderful his well was and how special and lifesaving it had become to the villagers. Ryan wanted to come to Uganda to see the well. It looked like he must raise more money.

Ryan went to the newspapers telling his story about the well project and how money was needed to go see the well and sample its clean water.

Funds started coming in from donations around Winnipeg. Ryan added this money to the funds he was earning until he had enough funds so he and his mom could fly to Africa and see his well. He was now nine years old.

When Ryan arrived in Uganda, the people in the little village were so grateful to see him that they lined up for miles on both sides of the only dirt road leading into their village. They were all clapping for Ryan as he got out of the rental car and walked by himself through this gauntlet of loving and admiring people.

"The Ryan's Well foundation provides access to clean water, sanitation, and hygiene education in the poorest regions of the world. They educate, motivate and inspire people to create the change what they want to see in the world."[104] As of April of 2018, Ryan's foundation has raised millions of dollars and installed over 1,166 water projects funded by Ryan's Well Foundation, 1,245 Latrines completed by Ryan's Well Foundation, and 892,725 people provided with clean water in 14 different countries.

Hannah Taylor, our previous hero of peace, started caring for her fellow man at five years old. Ryan Hreljac started his humanitarian programs at seven years old. I would say our future is in good hands if children can possess such caring hearts at such a young age.

The meaning of life is to find your gift. The purpose of life is to give it away.
Pablo Picasso

EFREN PENAFLORIDA
A Child Educating Slum Children
Profession: Student, fundraiser
Country: Philippines
Compassionate endeavor: Education for poor children

One personal characteristic that quickly identifies potential heroes is when someone sees something wrong, something that needs immediate improvement, and takes steps to correct the issue on his/her own. Efren Penaflorida is such a person.

---

104 Taken from the Ryan's Well website—mission statement—https://www.ryanswell.ca/GetWell/

Efren Penaflorida was born in 1981 in the Philippines. He grew up in an urban slum near a garbage dump in the city of Cavite. His father was a tricycle driver (taxi) and later started a small noodle business to help make ends meet.

As a child, Efren played in garbage dumps, swam in polluted water, and was often beat up by neighborhood street gangs. These gangs threatened to beat up children if they went to school. These same children were exempt from harm if they joined the gang. It was estimated in 2009, that over 130,000 children were members of urban street gangs in the Philippines.[105] Many children were recruited into these gangs as young as nine years old.

When Efren was sixteen years old, to fight the detrimental effect that gang violence was having on the area youth not attending school, he started the DTC (Dynamic Teen Company) at his high school. This organization started working on area high school campuses trying to discourage children from joining violent gangs. Helping the community through service projects and promoting personal growth was the mission of DTC. In 1997, Efren and his friends took DTC to the slums. There street children who did not or could not come to school found an alternative to joining gangs by attending Efren's "pushcart" school. Efren realized that if the slum children were afraid to come to school, he would take the school to the children. Efren took school supplies, books, chalk, black boards, tables, and chairs into poor areas of the city and set up portable classrooms in the streets where he worked with street kids every Saturday. Children in the slums loved this opportunity to learn in safety and swarmed Efren's portable-classroom cart when it arrived in their area. Most of the children attending Efren's school were between the ages of two and fourteen. Efren, and several of his volunteer friends, taught the slum children English, math, reading, and writing.

In addition to the portable classroom, Efren noticed how dirty the children were. He started a hygiene clinic where children can take a bath, learn about brushing their teeth, wearing clean clothes, and other sanitary living habits.

The DTC, like most start-up organizations, had initial difficulties financing their organization. Instead of just asking for donations, they now supplement their donation revenue by selling crafts they created and by recycling old bottles and newspapers.

---

105 My Heroes' Story Community, Amanda Molinaro, Page created on 7/31/2015 6:43:25 PM Efran Pennaflorida, Last edited 1/4/2017 11:50:00 PM https://myhero.com/ Efren_Penaflorida_2009

As of 2015, the DTC had helped over 1,500 slum children attending their push-cart classrooms. In addition to helping educate slum children, Efren and his volunteers have mentored former gang members and even counseled street addicts and school dropouts. Many of these former addicts and dropouts are now volunteers for DTC helping run the programs as well as raise money.

Efren stated, "I always tell my volunteers that you are the change that you dream, and I am the change that I dream. And collectively we are the change that this world needs to be."

Four pushcart classrooms are now providing service in the Philippine slums. They hope to have more classrooms carts in the future to help street children stay away from gangs and encourage them that learning is a very beneficial alternative.[106]

Despite these harsh conditions, Efren graduated from high school and went to college earning degrees in both computer technology and secondary education. Efren was named CNN Hero of the Year for 2009 which provided him with $100,000 cash to improve, promote, and continue his noble community service effort.[107]

---

106 Ibid
107 www.cnn.com/heroes

No one can make you feel inferior without your consent.
Eleanor Roosevelt

CHAPTER FOUR

The Values of Sustaining Self-Esteem and Showing Compassion

Sustaining Self-esteem

Enhance your self-esteem, not from the opinions of others, but from the compassionate causes you have chosen to embrace, and the perseverance and courage expended toward their resolve.

Displaying Compassion

Give simply to increase the amount of goodness in the world—often without recognition or reward. Give more to others than you receive in return, and carefully sustain this inequity as a distinctive characteristic of your leadership.

Heroes know that their background and circumstances may have influenced how they behave, but only they are responsible for whom they have become.
Unknown

You must be the change you wish to see in the world.
Mahatma Gandhi

There are two ways of exerting one's strength: one is pushing down, the other is pulling up.
Booker T. Washington

As a human being, possessing education, talent, and resources obligates you to help others less fortunate.
Arthur Saunders—Tuskegee Airman

I believe if you have assets others do not have (health, education, talents, resources, access to medical services), then it is your obligation as a human being to share those resources with those less fortunate. You might say there are two kinds of people in the world: those who have sufficient resources (food, water, shelter, medical care, education), and those who are in need. Compassion for others and recognition for who they are and what they have done is a fundamental principle of being human. This chapter profiles four heroes who gave freely of their own assets with no desire or expectation of receiving credit for their generosity: Hal Reichle, Glenys Halter, The Claw Lady, and the Flower Man.

HAL REICHLE, THE HERO OF ANONYMOUS GIVING
Profession: Student, soldier, helicopter pilot
City and Country: Bedford, Ohio, United States
Compassionate endeavor: Giving anonymously to strangers

Have you ever arrived home and found that someone anonymously weeded your garden? Going to the box office at a movie theater, have you ever found that your movie tickets were already paid by an unknown stranger? Would you be delightfully surprised if a waiter at your favorite restaurant brought you a card stating your dinner was already paid for including the tip? Welcome to the world of Hal Reichle (Rye kil), a hero of an extraordinary nature—a master of anonymity!

Giving anonymously is special. It eliminates the selfish reasons many people give to others such as receiving thanks, receiving recognition, or impressing others who may be watching. If no one sees you giving to another, if no one will ever hear or read about your good deed, if the recipient of your kindness does not know who their benefactor was, then you have truly given anonymously. Why should you do this?

Who Was Hal Reichle? What is SSSSH?
On February 20, 1991, Chief Warrant Officer Hal "Hooper" Reichle 27, was killed while piloting an OH-58 helicopter during the Desert Storm war. Hal was returning from a reconnaissance mission and reportedly entered a sandstorm resulting in his demise. Hal's death has started a slowly

spreading movement across the United States involving an anonymous and secret society performing anonymous good deeds for perfect strangers. Why? Who was Hal? Why did he have such an effect on people?

An Unusual Combination

When someone first heard about Hal Reichle and his giving nature, one often pictured a quiet, mild-mannered individual considering the priesthood as a calling. Upon learning that Hal was a rambunctious rascal with a love for life tantamount to Robin Hood, many people were somewhat mystified. Add to this contrast an Army helicopter pilot searching the Kuwaiti desert for the enemy knowing that only a few hours earlier he was behaving like a mischievous elf by secretly placing money in stranger's pockets in a crowded open-air market. Most busy public areas require diligence to deter pick pockets; with Hal your pockets may well find themselves replenished.

No, Hal Reichle was not a saint, but rather a cross between John Wayne and a leprechaun. He was filled with patriotism and loved America, yet he was an impish prankster, a devil-may-care adventurer, and never missed an opportunity to do everyday things in a most unconventional way. At a party, for example, instead of mixing the ingredients for a martini in a shaker, he would pour the ingredients into his mouth and then shake his head. Instead of calling a girl on the phone and inviting her out to dinner, a messenger would arrive at her door dressed as a Canterbury squire handing her a scribed invitation impaled on the end of a sword. Instead of washing a car on a warm and sunny day, Hal would wash his car during a gully-washer thunderstorm. "Saves water and creates an instant rinse." So, as you can see, Hal was intense, grandiose, and flamboyant during his quieter moments.

Hal appealed to everyone

Total strangers would like Hal within a few minutes of meeting him, but after half an hour of his effervescent personality, they would be hooked—they had a friend for life. To further illustrate this, Hal heard about a student at Hiram College (Hal's alma mater) that was turned down for a Guaranteed Student Loan by a Warren, Ohio bank. One hour later, Hal walked out of the bank's president's office shaking hands and laughing with the chief executive as they patted each other on the back. The student loan had been approved.

A Special Hidden Spirit

Inside this cavalier individual there was hidden a most unusual spirit, for Hal spent much of his time giving to others, anonymously. But when Hal gave his time or money to someone else, he did not write out a check and mail it to a charity. Instead most of Hal's good deeds involved planning, risk, and lots of adventure. Each act was a separate quest. Hal's deeds were deliberately made into a sport, a form of entertainment for himself, a personal undertaking rewarded by a special inner peace and satisfaction.

Occasionally we meet someone harboring the spirit of genuine, fundamental goodness. Such a rare individual is difficult to discern, for their gifts of love and kindness are often accomplished through their own initiatives, rather than through established channels at institutions like Hiram College. Such a person loves and honors almost everyone, not to please oneself or others, but simply because it enriches the world's goodness. We are not speaking of a devout missionary or a church representative, but rather someone having within them a measure of musketeer who makes the act of giving an exciting quest and a fun-filled adventure.

Hal Reichle was such a rare individual. To Hal, helping others was fun; it was the reason he was born. Friends, total strangers, millionaires, and the homeless became the recipient of Hal's simple goodness. An elderly woman awakened to find her lawn had been mysteriously mowed. A schoolteacher awakened and found her driveway shoveled free from snow. Someone else found his house freshly painted upon returning from vacation. A young mother and three-small children discovered they were "alleged" to be the 500th customer at the supermarket checkout line; therefore, their groceries were free. Several individuals, all temporarily short of funds, discovered bags of groceries at their front door. There was never a note left from anyone explaining serendipity's visit. Additional examples of Hal's genuine goodness are virtually endless. Rich or poor, you had an equal chance of being graced with Hal's adventures.

Examples of Hal's Escapades

While working at a warehouse to earn college money, Hal heard about a fellow worker whose car, a beaten-up old wreck, had broken down and was beyond fixing. The bank had just called informing Hal's co-worker he was turned down for a $2,000 loan for another used car because of poor credit and low income. He now had no way to drive to work and was in danger of losing his job. Five minutes after Hal's ten-minute coffee break, the co-worker received another call from the bank stating his loan had been approved. Next to the pay phone in the lunchroom was a telephone book opened to the page where the bank was listed. Next to the phone book was a freshly emptied coffee cup, still warm, depicting a picture of an Apache helicopter.

On a sunny Sunday morning, shortly after an elderly couple left their home for church, a pickup truck comically displaying temporary signs on its doors, arrived in the couple's driveway. Written in crayon on shirt cardboard, the signs read "Expert Lawn Service." Underneath these words in much smaller print was "Don't call us, we'll find you." During the next hour, Hal, with a borrowed lawn mower (the pick-up truck was borrowed too), cut and trimmed this couple's lawn. He was unshaven and wore a droopy fishing hat and sunglasses for disguise. An oversized, dark-blue work shirt, hanging open and unbuttoned, revealed a torn t-shirt with a picture of Big Bird from Sesame Street. Hal slowly shuffled behind the lawn mower like a tired, hunchbacked worker. If you listened carefully over the sound of the mower, you could have heard frequent giggling accompanied by a little skip or two-step in Hal's walk, which betrayed his subterfuge for those astute enough to notice. Then, just before the couple returned from church, our makeshift gardener disappeared as quickly as he had arrived.

Carefully Planned Good Deeds—A Question of Legality

How did Hal know when this couple went to church? How did he know when they were to return? How did he know they didn't have their own lawn service? How did Hal know the snowy driveway belonged to a schoolteacher? Who did Hal know at the bank to get the car loan approved? The point being is Hal's anonymous acts of kindness were not random, but carefully planned and executed within specified time frames. Some of his escapades took weeks of planning. Others were more spontaneous.

Stalking people to watch their movements and learn of their activities is usually illegal. Such actions are often associated with predators, burglars, and kidnappers. Such actions are also associated with careful planners of anonymous good deeds. Is it against the law to stalk the activities of an elderly couple so you can cut their grass while they are attending church? It might very well be, not to mention trespassing on their property while cutting their grass. As previously mentioned, one couple returned from vacation to find their modest house had been freshly painted. There was some stalking and trespassing involved with that good deed to be sure.

I've heard rumors of the police, at 3:30 a.m. on a foggy Wednesday morning, unsuccessfully chased a prowler from the back yard of a private home. Being unable to apprehend the fleeing suspect, the police returned to the house to check for clues. They found twenty-five freshly planted flowers, two empty flats, one flat filled with twelve Johnny Jump-ups, and a small garden spade. Three blocks away, emerging from the mist, there came a jogger running at a slow to moderate pace along the sidewalk used by many joggers in the community. This jogger, for an unknown reason, was giggling and wearing a pair of gardening gloves. As he jogged around the corner, he discarded his gloves in a garden of wildflowers and mountain laurel growing on the corner lot. His giggling continued—go figure.

Checking Out an Area

Most of us drive to work thinking about the day's activities ahead of us. Hopefully we notice the spring flowers and the sunrise on our way and the sunset on our return. As Hal Reichle drove along, he not only noticed the sunsets and flowers, but also carefully studied the surrounding area. His head would fill with little notes: that garage needs painting; that house needs flowers; that person could probably use some groceries, that yard needs mowing.

Hal's lust for life, fun, adventure, and for being a harmless prankster are cavalier qualities that, when mixed with his natural goodness and his love for mankind, created a most unusual man. As noted, Hal also possessed Robin Hood characteristics, (not the stealing part) and several times his adventures required many of his friends to accompany him—his band of merry men. Hal also had an enchanted elf-like quality about him, seeming to know things through premonition alone, often disappearing like a ninja, and frequently accomplishing things one would think required magic—a most intriguing, mysterious, and wonderful individual.

Carrying On the Magical Tradition—SSSSH

Hal is a perfect example of how a controversial rascal, one likely to be reprimanded for setting off fire crackers or toilet-papering a tree on Halloween, can still harbor a loving and giving heart. Perhaps we should all possess less of a tendency to judge others, for there may be many mischievous scalawags out there possessing a spirit of gold.

How did Hal have such influence over people? I can only state that Hal's personality carried about it an easily detected glow of safety and reassurance. It somehow exuded great trust and a peaceful feeling of well-being. Even more remarkable was a magical sense of warmth and wonderment that simmered within the hearts of people when Hal was around, as if the aura from an enchanted sorcerer's incantation was enshrouding them with virtue.

Always smiling, usually laughing, frequently clowning around with his silly antics, Hal made everyone he met feel good about themselves. Mystifying to be sure; I suspect even magical—as if a frolicking sprite whose destiny was to show others how to spread goodness by creating fun-filled and adventurous exploits. If true; it worked!

When Hal was killed in 1991, I decided to continue his anonymous giving to others coupled with his sense of adventure. In this way, Hal's good deeds would continue, and his loving spirit would live on to benefit the lives of thousands. After I formed SSSSH (Secret Society of Serendipitous Service to Hal) in 2003, thousands of people started to do anonymous good deeds for total strangers in Hal's spirit. This participation resulted because of publicity from CNN, Good Morning America, People Magazine, The Discovery Channel, and other magazines and radio and television stations. SSSSH is also soliciting your participation. What a wonderful tribute to an almost mystical person, Hal Reichle, a man from which legends are made. See http://ssssh.org.

Ego-Free Compassion = Performing acts of generosity, charity, and kindness for strangers, anonymously, without receiving satisfaction, recognition, or reward from any source other than from deep within; giving simply for the intent of increasing the amount of goodness in the world.

Hiram College Scholarship

The measure of one's love for humanity does not manifest itself through words or feelings, but rather in behavior. Thus, it is one's demonstrated generosity, understanding, compassion, kindness, and guiding hand that exhibit one's willingness to love his fellowman.

The Hal Reichle Memorial Award is not based on perfect class attendance, and it is not based on financial need. One's acts of kindness serve as a major indicator of an individual's qualifications for this scholarship. The recipient is chosen for his/her humanitarian efforts, community involvement, and volunteerism. Thus, it is in one's behavior—the generosity, understanding compassion, kindness, and guiding hand—that exhibits one's willingness to love, and one's unique and rare qualifications for this award. Hence, applications for the scholarship do not exist.

This is a two-faceted award comprising a tuition grant plus an enrichment component that should lead to further discovery and growth. The award is void of any considerations regarding sex, race, religion, national origin, sexual orientation, or other similar, inconsequential attributes. The award is not always given each year, for understandably, qualified recipients cannot always be located. When the Award Committee is successful, however, a very rare individual has been found. This recipient, harboring a heart of simple goodness, is destined to enrich scores of peoples' lives. Know him well, or know her well, and your life will be positively enriched from the experience.

Hiram College president addresses scholarship dinner

This speech was given on May 7, 2003, at the Hiram College Hal Reichle Memorial Scholarship Award's Dinner by Richard Scaldini, President of Hiram College.

Good evening and welcome to Hiram College.

It is my great pleasure to welcome the members of Hal Reichle's family who have created this unique scholarship. I also want to commend Eric Buckman and the past recipients who have joined us this evening. Each of you reaffirms the values that Hal Reichle represented and each of you sheds a favorable light on our institution. To the members of our community and friends of Hiram, thank you for joining us to remember an outstanding individual and his successors.

There are images and experiences that warm your heart and tickle your funny bone. I am thinking of children's excitement on Christmas morning, or surprise parties, or reunions. They are not only moments of deep feeling, but fun, surprising, and humorous. An outstanding example is what I have decided to name the Reichle Stratagem. It is an action that is designed to achieve at one and the same time: a kindness, a surprise, a gesture of caring, and to inspire delight on the part of both doer and recipient. The Reichle Stratagem does not make one think of the great saints and ascetics; rather, it makes one think of the Three Musketeers and Robin Hood. It is a form of giving that unquestionably springs from pure motives and the kind of selflessness that enhances the life of the benefactor as much as the beneficiary. It embodies what the ancient Christians called "caritas," the etymological root of charity: that is: love in its highest form. But that isn't a sufficient characterization. You should imagine this figure of Pauline spirituality working his magic like a Halloween prankster.

The Reichle Stratagem is built on secrecy. Secrecy ensures selflessness: that is, a complete focus on the goodness of the act rather than on the character of the actor. It sends a message to the beneficiary that the thought behind the gesture is entirely for the recipient, that there is no ulterior motive. It has all the characteristics of a prank but lacks any suggestion of meanness.

The Reichle Stratagem is a weapon in the war against human solitude. Out of the blue, you discover that someone is thinking about you; that someone cares; that someone sees your need and responds.

There is something quintessentially "Hiram" about the Reichle Stratagem. First and foremost, it is about service to others and the community. This goes to the College's mission: the preparation of students for citizenship and leadership in their communities. A fundamental dimension of education is the movement beyond the self to the discovery of the world and others. As I have said, the Reichle Stratagem begins with selflessness. Acts of selflessness make citizens out of individuals; they elevate humans to humanity.

Most important, the Reichle Stratagem is fun. Fun in the doing; delight in the surprise. We forget too often the importance of humor to the great humanists: think of Shakespeare and Rabelais. Humor reminds us that, as individuals, we share in the greatness of humankind but that we are not the sum of the world. Humor in charity offers a gentle and lightening response to need; it humanizes the good life, making it clear that goodness is within reach of us all.

These are virtues, and a form of virtue, that Hiram wishes to instill in its students. The Reichle Stratagem is an experience that we wish to weave into the fabric of our community. Community: it is a word that one hears everywhere at Hiram. We define much of our distinctiveness as an institution in terms of the community that we create. And it is created and re-created every day. Now, you can't have a community of one. It begins with the involvement of one individual in the life of another. You might say that Hiram's community is built on the Reichle Stratagem.

I offer you these reflections as a way of thanking the Reichle family for institutionalizing the caring, mischievous, selfless character of Hal Reichle in this scholarship. I thank them for their generosity, and I thank them for giving Hiram a living, renewable embodiment of the values we stand for.

The World-wide SSSSH Crusade

The SSSSH movement took off like a rocket with kind-hearted people all over the world performing anonymous acts of kindness for total strangers. Participants wrote me about their anonymous good deeds not only from every state in the Union, but from Africa, France, Germany, Switzerland, and many other countries. From kindergarten children cleaning the chalkboard erasers for the teacher, to native American children on reservations doing good deeds for a school project, to members of our military service spreading joy around the world. This chapter contains a small fraction of the many letters and emails I have received. Enjoy!

What follows is a few of the hundreds of letters sent to SSSSH from anonymous givers. (These letters are unedited for spelling and grammar)

An ongoing anonymous act of kindness

On snowy days when I leave work, I don't only clear off my car, but the car next to me.

Reichle was described as a rascal by Roger Cram. He would appreciate this: Years ago, I spotted a lonely bare weed growing thorough a crack at the intersection of State Route. 77 and Brookpark Road. This weed looked like a stripped-down Christmas tree. It was just over a week until Christmas. So very late one night, I believe it was about 2:am I proceeded to decorate it with bulbs and roping. I hope it brighten a few people over the next week.

The only other deed is a poor woman to whom I delivered Meals-on-Wheels. She is a paraplegic and one of her pleasures was watching the Cleveland Indians on TV, but this past year they were only on cable, which she could not afford. Had cable brought to her. Hope to do more.

Anonymous Good Deeds done in the loving memory of Hal Reichle

When it's a windy day, or perhaps a garbage man has been hurried and over worked, and I'm driving down "that street," I stop, no matter what, and place the "can in the street" on the lawn of the house of its rightful owner. On a very windy day, that may mean several inconvenient stops. No one sees me, nobody need know, right Hal? God blesses every good deed with secret grace.

I was driving back to the Cleveland area from Pittsburgh, and I anonymously paid tolls for the drivers behind me. I did that at two tollbooths. It's not much, but I hope the people who didn't have to pay their tolls were pleasantly surprised.

When putting flowers on the graves of my parents, I noticed the grave of a boy who died of heart disease when we were in the 7th grade, more than four decades ago. Knowing his family would arrive within days to decorate his grave for Memorial Day, I wrote a note to the boy, telling him I remembered how beautiful and nice he was and that I would never forget him. I mounted it to a stick and stuck it in the ground by his stone where his loved ones would find it and know they weren't the only ones who mourned him after all these years. I did it for the family. I did it for Hal.

After leaving the restaurant, I bought four boxes of Popsicles and handed them out at the student union on our local campus. That's 53 people who benefited from Hal's kindness on Sunday!

On Monday (three days before thanksgiving I went to the grocery to pick up some last-minute items, seeing a woman there with the 3 children in tow I heard each one ask again and again for items they wanted and heard Mommy say NO we CANT afford that, they were asking for cookies crackers and macaroni and cheese... I looked a bit closer and saw though they were clean the clothing was worn and did not fit well ... I went to the store manager and bought 250.00 worth of store gift certificates and handed them to the manager along with a card from your group and showed him who to give them to. He smiled like a child and added another 50 to my gift and handed the lady the card, as she was checking out, she cried,, and told the kids to go get the cookies they wanted, cause now she can pay the electric and phone AND feed the kids. Thanksgiving was a lot happier at my home this year, she made me feel better just knowing she was able to feed and keep her little ones warm. Thanks Hal... you are an inspiration.

It was about two months ago, my wife, myself, and two other couples were eating at a Chinese restaurant in Nashville, TN. The waitress told us that she would bring us our bill, but someone had already paid it. We couldn't believe it, because the bill had to be about $150 for the six of us, plus one child. We debated this all night. Some thought it was the waitress, while others of us tried to figure out who would have done it. You see, myself and one of the other men that night, are blind, so we really weren't certain what the motive was. We never had been able to figure anything out, but I think your story on Good Morning America has just told me everything. I know we'll probably never know who committed that unexpected act of kindness, but on behalf of everyone there, I would simply like to say "Thank you."

THIS HAS TOUCHED MY HEART!!!
I heard about this on Good Morning America just now!
I CRIED!!
Thank God for people like you all!
I just went out and purchased a $100. gift cert. from Price Chopper and am on my way now to give it (SSSSH) to a single mom and her children.
I can't wait!
Just printed out your cards on this web site
HOW COOL!!
Thank you for continuing acts of kindness
Please count me in!!!!
IN MEMORY OF HAL!
With Love, Me:

I would just like to say that ever since I can remember, I have been looking for something in my life that would make others smile. I feel that we are put on this earth for a reason, and I could never figure out what my reason was. I saw this on Good Morning America, and at that instant, I knew what I was going to do in my life to help others. When you have a bad situation, like what happened to Hal, you need to find a way to make some good out it, and this is it. You have helped me with finally figuring out why I was put here and what I need to do...I can't thank you enough and just wanted you to know that. I can't wait to get started.

In honor of Hal Reichle, we gave $100 gift certificate to Giant Eagle anonymously to a woman with 5 children (who lives paycheck-to-paycheck) so she and her family could enjoy a nice Christmas dinner. Happy Holidays to all and God Bless!

Hi, I am a seventh grader at Maize South Middle School in Kansas. My English teacher put together an assignment that had to do with joining your club. We all had to do an anonymous good deed. It was very special experience for me, and I wanted you to hear what I did. My family and I were coming back from Austin, Texas for Thanksgiving and I decided to pay for the toll for the person behind me. We were just entering Andover before I could give the money. I wrote a card and put the money inside. I then gave it to the toll woman, and she thought it was the nicest thing. We pulled forward and drove slowly. They were so surprised! As we turned into our neighborhood they honked and waved as they drove by. It was really cool, and I hope you enjoy my story.

Problems with anonymous giving

Giving anonymously offers spectacular yet heart-warming benefits. It provides a wonderful opportunity to get closer to yourself, to truly learn who you are, to establish a peaceful intimacy with your essence. Giving anonymously also provides a way the poor can give to others making the indigent feel special about themselves in an area not usually touched.

I received a phone call from a sheriff's department in Florida complaining about a brand-new bicycle that was left on an elementary school ground for one of the children. As it turns out, an anonymous lady drove to work every day passing a child riding a beat-up bicycle to school. The bicycle was in such poor condition, that twice she witnessed the front wheel fall off forcing the student to carry the bike. Wanting to do a SSSSH good deed, she bought a new bicycle and locked it to the old bicycle at the bike racks on the school property. She fastened a SSSSH card to the new bike. The young boy found the new bike fastened to his old one, did not fully understand the gesture, and inquired about it with one of his teachers. The teacher, understanding even less than the boy, called the sheriff's department complaining about someone trespassing on the school property. The sheriff deputy, looking at the SSSSH card left on the new bike, looked up the SSSSH website and called me in Ohio. The deputy was bitterly complaining about one of my employees walking on the school property without permission. I attempted to explain to the deputy the loving principles of SSSSH, but my efforts fell on deaf ears. You will just never know.

As you plan your anonymous giving escapades, keep in mind the possible feelings and rights of your recipients as you try to make this unusual and kind gesture a positive experience for them. Taking these precautions with your anonymous giving gestures, will have the best of hopes, the purest of intentions, the raw goodness of human compassion. Armed with such magnificence, you will never fail your anonymous giving adventures, even if they are not entirely welcomed by the recipient. Enjoy the journeys!

The basis of SSSSH is giving to total strangers anonymously. This is a complex phenomenon riddled with surprising manifestations. One engaging in this activity for the first time might experience an unsatisfied and somewhat empty feeling that follows his or her first few anonymous good deeds. Why?

One's ego and self-esteem benefits through peer recognition of one's accomplishments. Such reinforcement also improves one's confidence and encourages personal growth, but how does this internal benefit occur when giving anonymously?

Giving to others with "ego-free compassion" may cause some internal-reward problems for someone just starting to do anonymous good deeds. Where's your pat-on-the-back? Where are the compliments from your peers acknowledging your unselfishness and generosity? Where's that grateful tone in your recipient's voice accompanied by the happy, sparkle-eyed excitement that makes you feel so good about what you've done? When giving anonymously, you might feel a little empty, unfulfilled, and even a little disappointed. Don't be discouraged, for a wondrous essence is starting to emerge within you.

Now, when you are able, go do another anonymous good deed. Make sure you're alone. Afterwards, sit quietly again. You'll notice the stirring within you is stronger now, more discernible, and it seems to be accompanied by a curious peacefulness.

As you might suspect, a third anonymous good deed is suggested followed by another intimate session with your internal serenity. The deep stirring is again more noticeable and is the awakening of your "ego-free compassion."

Anonymously creating more goodness in the world just for the sake of creating more goodness, that's what SSSSH is all about—giving without your ego. It is a complex, private, and internally cherished undertaking. It takes practice, study, and reflection as do many gratifying accomplishments.

A paraplegic in California needed a van with hand controls, since his feet could not operate a brake or accelerator. He refused all charity most emphatically, but when the keys and title to a hand-controlled van were left in an envelope on the altar of his church, the anonymity of the gesture allowed him to accept the gift without feeling obligated to any individual(s). Sometimes anonymity is the only way.

Remember, SSSSH is a "Secret Society." It's not only a secret because our members and their good deeds are anonymous, but also because it is difficult to describe to anyone the resulting intimacy with your ego-free compassion. These wonderful perceptions remain within your internal serenity for only you to revere.

SSSSH is also a "Serendipitous Service," and this will become most apparent as you continue performing anonymous good deeds (SSSSHing). Your selected recipients will benefit most remarkably from your anonymous kindnesses, as if they were carefully chosen through a detailed and tedious selection process. Perhaps they were.

If you are now a member or will soon become a member of SSSSH, welcome to the magic, maintain your stealth, partake in many enchanted adventures, and have a delightfully wondrous life. But remember, there will be few thank-you notes or recognitions, for SSSSH is truly a secret.

Give of yourself to increase the amount of goodness in the world,
not to receive recognition from others for your deeds.
Hal "Hooper" Reichle

GLENYS VAN HALTER
Rescuing Children from their Abusers—Rotary Assisted
Profession: School teacher
City and Country: Cape Town, South Africa
Compassionate endeavor: The rescue and education of poor
and abused children

To say Glenys is a determined woman is like saying a shark's feeding frenzy is tantamount to an English afternoon tea. I believe she is driven by forces so powerful that the devil triple-locks his gate when Glenys is rumored to be in his area. And what's most amazing and serendipitous to mankind is that her incredible ambition and energy is channeled solely to benefit the destitute.

The time this writing depicts is 2004. I enter a suburb in South Africa called Khayelitsha (Ki a leash a), a township outside of Cape Town consisting of over one million[108] people living in corrugated tin shacks without plumbing and where there is one public water faucet for every 600 people. I looked around this area. I saw no little animals running about like squirrels,

---

108 Reliefweb, October 10, 2017, A person-centered approach to preventing HIV in Khayelitsha's children, International HIV/AIDS Alliance

rabbits, rats, or mice. Anything that moves, I was told by Glenys, is eaten. I looked around again. I did not see any trees or shrubs—for anything that grows is burned for cooking and warmth.

It appears the natural instincts for the protection of one's own young are often overruled by the male-dominant bonds in a family structure. They are so extreme that intrafamily violence is perceived as a necessity for survival. Many cultures in Africa consider women and children to be almost without value, leaving their fate to the whims of uneducated and

Glenys van Halter shows shirts made by students (see also page 137).

often intoxicated males. In Khayelitsha, with their 60% HIV/AIDS infestation in 2004, superstition encouraged men to have sex with a virgin believing their HIV/AIDS could be cured or prevented by the act itself purifying their blood. As a result, many young girls, and children as young as three months were raped.[109]

Other men raped women to maintain their masculinity because living in Khayelitsha provides little opportunity for males to support their families and maintain their self-esteem.[110] It is a very frightening culture for many. For outsiders, this extreme hardship is difficult to comprehend without seeing and experiencing it.

The former South African Apartheid government prohibited blacks from living in cities by passing its 1950 Group Areas Act. Hundreds of thousands of blacks were forced to break up their families and communities and move out of cities like Cape Town so these urban locations could become white cosmopolitan areas. Many of the dislodged black citizens became nomads.[111]

---

109 From a personal interview in 2004 with Hero of Peace Reverend Corine McClintock, Sparrow Village, Chapter Thirteen of this book, Value of Perseverance.
110 From Wikipedia, the free encyclopedia, HIV/AIDS in South African townships, Rape as a Cure, Sexual Violence
111 *SAHO (South African History Online) Group Area Act of 1950* http://www.sahistory.org.za/article/group-areas-act-1950

After the defeat of the Apartheid government in 1994 (See hero Nelson Mandela), blacks could move back into urban areas searching for work. Many became squatters as they erected shacks made of tin, wood, and cardboard on any unoccupied land—Khayelitsha is one of these areas. There are many such townships in Africa. Close to ten million people try to scratch out a bleak existence by living in one of these challenging townships.[112] Count your breaths for the next year; you will reach close to ten million.[113] Can you comprehend that each breath represents a human life trying to survive in near chaos in a South African township?

Glenys was going blind
Glenys had terrible vision. One eye was totally blind, and the other eye was poor. She went to an eye surgeon who informed her she would be totally blind within a few months from a degenerative eye condition. The surgeon then stated he has invented a new surgical technique that might help, but he has never performed the operation before. The surgeon suggested the new operation be tried on Glenys's blind eye. In that way if it does not work, her sight will not be any worse off than it is. Glenys agreed.

Miraculously as it might seem, the blind eye's operation resulted in 100% restoration of Glenys's eyesight, 20-20, so the same experimental operation was performed on her other eye with the same amazing result. Glenys asked her doctor how she could possibly pay him for these miracles? The doctor replied, "Go out into the world and do good. Report to me in one year with evidence of your humanitarian endeavors. I will evaluate your efforts at that time and determine your payment, if any, for my services.[114]

All the unattended children on the streets
Glenys knew about the HIV/AIDS superstition promoted by the many witchdoctors working in Khayelitsha. She knew the many small children, abandoned to the streets during the day when their mothers were working, were molested by fathers, brothers, uncles, and other men of great ignorance and ill repute. Glenys believed that if a school could be built for the children, it would benefit them in two ways: (1) They would receive a critically needed education, and (2) They would be kept off the streets and safe from the molesters for much of the daytime hours.

---

112 *Business Tech*, August 14, 2016, *these are the biggest townships in South Africa*, https://businesstech.co.za/news/general/132269/these-are-the-biggest-townships-in-south-africa/
113 At rest, I, Roger Cram, breathe twenty times per minute = 1,200 times per hour = 28,800 times per day = 10,512,000 breaths per year
114 The author obtained this information in 2004 from a personal one-day interview with Glenys van Halter in Khayelitsha, South Africa.

How does one start a school in South Africa?

What qualifications and other requirements must be met before a school can be approved by the Board of Education in South Africa? What zoning laws pertain to school construction in Khayelitsha? What permits, licenses, building codes, and training are required by South Africa and local townships to start a school? Could Glenys obtain these needed credentials?

I am sure many of my readers are familiar with the legend of the Pied Piper of Hamelin where all the children in Hamelin, Germany, were marched out of town by the enchanting and captivating tunes from the Pied Piper. Well, Glenys did not have a magic flute, but she did not need one as she entered the back alleys of Khayelitsha and commandeered children, (eighteen to be exact) by singing a song and skipping along as she went. Glenys invited children to join her playful parade and lead them to a shaded tree on an empty lot. Here she proceeded to teach these eager children, starving for attention and knowledge, the subjects of music, English, art, and history.[115]

The odd thing about the occurrence is not the abduction of eighteen children, but rather the tree. Remember, everything that grows in Khayelitsha is burned for cooking or fuel to stay warm. Wooden telephone poles are no longer used by utility companies because they are cut down by citizens for fuel shortly after erected. Where did this fully-grown tree come from? How did it escape the fate of other vegetation?

Glenys returned to the tree the next day and found twenty-four students waiting for her intellectual gifts. The following day forty-eight students anxiously awaited her loving attention.

It was obvious that a school was desperately needed in Khayelitsha. Glenys started going door-to-door asking for donations and inquiring about any certified teachers that may be living in the area. She went to businesses within and without the township area pleading for help. She went to the owner of the empty lot where the mysterious tree presided, and found it was owned by a church. The first time Glenys approached the church authorities, they had no interest in donating their land for a school. They remained uninterested the second through the tenth time Glenys contacted them. As time passed, Glenys recruited many interested parties and donations to support her project. Many of her volunteers were members of the church's congregation that owned the land. Pressure to surrender the land gradually started to build from the many church parishioners. Finally, on Glenys's twentieth visit to the church authorities, they surrendered the land to her school. This gift was probably to stop her hounding them as much as the good intentions of the church.[116]

---

115 Ibid
116 Ibid

Glenys was successful in starting her school. She built four classroom buildings, a library, a playground, and a vegetable garden that not only taught the children farming but also provided food for their school meals. When Glenys showed me the school vegetable garden, it was surrounded in barbed wire. "These fresh vegetables are too tempting for a surrounding population in need of food!" Glenys informed me.

The best innovation of all was a merry-go-round on the playground that the children spun around as they hung on for their delight. Hidden

inside the merry-go-round was a water pump attached to a well. When the children played on the device, they pumped water up to a water tower only a few feet away. The water tower was connected to a bathroom building housing four flush toilets, the only flush toilets within a five-mile radius. Glenys had to not only teach classes in arithmetic and reading, but also in how to use flush toilets as well. As I viewed the four-toilet bathroom, I noticed they were bolted to the ground with iron straps to prevent theft during the night. A vegetable garden with barbed wire and toilets bolted to the wall with iron straps—I was receiving an education about surviving in Khayelitsha! Glenys was educating me as well as her 600 students!

At the time I interviewed Glenys, most of the teachers in her school were volunteers from the neighborhood interested in providing an education for all the disadvantaged children. The education they provided must be a high quality because Glenys informed me her school was authorized and certified by the South Africa Board of Education and her graduating students were passing the South Africa Standardized test.

Nine-year old prostitutes

I imagine it is difficult for many readers of this book to envision nine-year old prostitutes and how desperate conditions must be to necessitate this extreme measure, but I assure you, it is most prevalent throughout the world. Glenys knew many young girls attending her school were involved in the sex trade. To help them earn a living and get off the streets, Glenys started a sewing-craft school in the back room of her house. Her young girls, under Glenys's loving and patient instruction, learned to make clothes, jewelry, place mats, and other crafts that the children could sell and support themselves enough, so their prostitution activities were not necessary.

I examined many of the jackets, shirts, and other clothing made by Glenys's youngest entrepreneurs. I found them comparable to the quality of clothing sold in stores. I was amazed!

The brothel

Into the twisted back alleys in this land of festering immoralities there is a brothel. Large rocks rest upon the tin roof to keep the wind from blowing the building apart. A door of corrugated tin separates a three-year-old child from her immoral customers. Her mother, however, has trained her three-year-old daughter to please men in a sick and perverted fashion, being the only means of support for this woman and her other nine children.

Glenys rescues a three-year old

It is night. It is dark. There is a fire burning in a metal drum in front of this brothel providing light so deranged customers can find their way. Suddenly, with a piercing gong, the corrugated tin door flies open slamming against the shack's metal walls. The entire structure shakes with haunting oscillations dislodging some of the rocks upon the roof. Five startled men quickly stand up, draw their weapons, and train them upon a silhouetted figure now occupying the doorway.

"Give me that child!" Glenys ordered pointing to the three-year-old girl standing at her mother's feet. This command, although most earnest and with ample volume, did not diminish the metal latching sounds of five weapons being cocked into their firing mode.

"I've told the police and the news media that I'm here. Shoot me and they'll all have you for dinner! Now, give me that child!"

Glenys reached out and grabbed the three-year-old girl and then raced out the door. It was like she was never there having used swiftness and surprise to her best and possibly only advantage. Miraculously, no gun shots were heard. The girl's mother appeared in the door shouting, "Bring her back. She is my only way to make money. How will I support my family!?"

Glenys shouted back as she jumped in her little rusted car clinching the child to her chest, "Find another way!" Upon reaching her beat-up car, Glenys put the child in a wicker laundry basket on the front passenger seat and prayed her car would start.

Did Glenys escape this ordeal?

There was little electricity available in Khayelitsha; therefore, there were no streetlights, no traffic lights, and no lights coming from the thousands of shanties. Only the warm glow of many fires and oil lamps competed poorly against Glenys's one misaligned headlight. Many of the alleys and byways only existed because no tin shack occupied their space; therefore, it was a long and twisted route to the eventual end of the township, and there were no street signs to serve as a guide.

As Glenys sped along the congested dirt alleys filled with garbage and potholes, she concentrated on her rear-view mirror. Her little car could not outrun anyone giving chase, and if she drove any faster, she would break an axle from encountering the many holes, rocks, and debris along her escape route. A broken axle would make Glenys easy prey for the many hidden and inquisitive eyes that so curiously followed her every movement. Five minutes had passed, and Glenys estimated she was over one mile away from the brothel, but still deep inside the frightening township! This was no place for a woman, especially a white woman alone at night!

Glenys was worried as the brazen act she just committed began to register. She had stolen a child, kidnapped it right in front of the child's mother, in defiance of the law and the five guns trained upon her! "Civil disobedience at its finest!" she said to herself convinced that her blatant act of raw courage, laced with total disregard for consequences, has saved the child's life.

What does her escape route look like?

There are few designated roads. The dusty and pothole-filled alleys are muddled with constant turns and dead-end alleyways. Glenys quickly turned right only to find she had just entered a cul-de-sac with a corrugated-tin shanty at the end. Slamming on her brakes to avoid hitting the shack, her car sputtered to a stop with the engine quitting a few feet from the hut. It was quiet. It was very dark. There were no lights coming from within the structure. The dirt and debris disrupted by her sudden stop occupied her one headlight's beam aiming slightly up and to the right. Much to the delight of predators prowling this area, Glenys's twisted headlight was serving as an unwanted beacon betraying her location. The dust soon joined the evening breeze clearing the air around her. She quickly turned off her headlight to seek more concealment. She knew, sitting there motionless and terrified, that the darkness and silence were her only allies, but how fickle these allies were, for as each second passed, they gradually switched loyalties from those hiding to those who hunt.

Glenys slowly raised her eyes toward the rear-view mirror afraid of what she might see. She knew she had to try and start her car, but what if it would not start? A repeated grinding sound of a car that will not start would send a message of vulnerable prey into the darkness. For a second, Glenys considered fleeing the area on foot running between the dark shanties toward the distant city lights. What should she do?

The frightened and bewildered three-year-old child, still in the laundry basket, started to cry—loudly. Glenys saw approaching headlights a few alleys over toward the brothel, and a flicker of fire came from within the shanty next to her as the corrugated front door started to open. The decision was made! Glenys immediately attempted to start her little car, but forgetting it was in gear, the car lunged forward striking the shanty with a disconcerting crash, breaking her one headlight, forcing the shanty door closed, and forcing the person opening it inward to the floor. The child screamed louder. The oncoming headlights grew closer. Glenys pushed in the clutch, started the car, put it in reverse, backed away from the shanty, turned the car around, and headed toward alley's opening just as the car with the approaching headlights passed by. Were these the men from the brothel chasing her? They were going extremely fast. Because she was off the main dirt alleys and without any working headlights, they apparently did not see her.

Glenys followed the people that were chasing her

Glenys decided her only way out of the township was to follow that speeding car. Without any streetlights and no headlights, the only possible way to navigate was to stay close to the taillights of this speeding car. Glenys decided she would be going the right direction if she were heading toward the distant city lights of Cape Town, but she could barely keep up. She couldn't see where she was driving in the darkness, but she knew if she stayed close enough to that car ahead of her, she wouldn't hit anything unless they hit it first. "Am I really following men with guns who want to kill me?" Glenys exclaimed to herself in dismay. "If they look behind them, I'm dead, but I hope they're looking for my taillights ahead of them."

The ride was very bumpy with frequent turns skidding around corners in the dirt roads. Glenys hit her head on the roof many times and the screaming child popped out of and back into the laundry basket. After what must have been the ride of a lifetime, streetlights were ahead as the speeding car left the Khayelitsha darkness and entered the main streets of Cape Town. For fear of discovery from the city lights, Glenys dropped far back and stopped in the darkness on a dirt road. There she waited in silence until the car ahead had disappeared.

Glenys turned the child over to the authorities, and she was placed with a caring foster family within a few days.[117] Of course, as you might have suspected, the mother of the three-year old child will simply take her four-year-old child from her family into the brothel and repeat this horrifying process again. So, one girl-child was saved and another endangered in her place! Will Glenys rescue this other child in the future? Is there a limit to her courage?

I'm sure you understand different cultures, especially third world developing countries, have limited public services often requiring harsher actions by those addressing a crisis. Do you think Glenys, if in the United States, could pick up eighteen children off the streets to start a school under a tree? Do you think Glenys could get away with raiding a brothel and stealing a three-year old child?

THE CLAW LADY
Enchantress of Khayelitsha, South Africa—Rescuing New Orphans
Profession: Veterinarian
City and Country: Khayelitsha, South Africa
Compassionate endeavor: Locating starving orphan children

In 2004, Khayelitsha, South Africa, was an extremely poor township. It still is. The ghetto consisted mostly of corrugated tin shacks. HIV virus was very prevalent with many deaths occurring, especially of parents. A

---

117 The author obtained this information in 2004 from a personal one-day interview with Glenys van Halter in South Africa as she gave me a tour of her school, her house, and the neighborhood.

true tragedy occurs when the parents, or more often the only parent, dies of HIV leaving behind several children. It is not uncommon for all these children to be under ten years of age. When the only parent of such a family dies from HIV, the remaining children have no means of support or survival. If the oldest child is near ten years of age, that child becomes the only hope for his/her siblings. If they have a family dog, and many families do, the dog is the first to be without food and water.

One day in 2003, an emaciated dog (you could count the ribs) was picked up off the streets of Khayelitsha by a good Samaritan who brought it to a lady veterinarian for care (I do not know the vet's name). The veterinarian was concerned how the dog got that way, because if a family could not afford to feed their dog, they might not be able to feed their children either. The veterinarian, seeing that the dog was friendly, believed it to be from a family instead of being a wild dog roaming the neighborhood for scraps of food.

The veterinarian took the dog back to the area where it was found and turned it loose. The veterinarian knew it might return to its home. That is exactly what happened. Upon finding the dog's home, the veterinarian also found six children, all under ten years of age, two in diapers, three sick, and the mother dead on the bed. The children were very hungry, were wearing filthy rags, and there was no available water.

The veterinarian made arrangements for the children to be bathed, given water, given medical attention, and fed. The dog was cared for as well. Between relatives and good neighbors, all six children and the dog were found suitable homes.

This veterinarian decided to dedicate her time to finding children whose parents have died leaving them abandoned. The way the veterinarian was going to go about this was finding the homes of wandering emaciated dogs and checking on the children living there. This methodology can only benefit starving children who have a withered dog. The destitute children without pets unfortunately did not benefit from this good fortune.

The Claw-Lady legend starts
Stories started spreading because it was rumored she was following emaciated dogs. The neighborhood named her the Claw Lady. The destitute children she locates are fed, given medical care, furnished with clothing, sent to school, and provided with future arrangements for their care. When neighbors or relatives cannot be found to care for these starving kids, the children mysteriously receive food and water delivered to their shack for weeks and months to come. It is my understanding, although

the children are still left alone under the last scenario, they are better off than being placed in homes through government agencies. I suspect the Claw Lady has a network of volunteers highly skilled in humanitarian and clandestine procedures. I am sure that agents of this secret network make frequent health-check visits to these selected homes.

I slowly drove around the dirt streets of Khayelitsha for several hours looking for any sign of the Claw Lady. Glenys van Halter, one of the peaceful heroes previously discussed, was with me. But Glenys and I were not sure what we were looking for. Is the Claw Lady a Caucasian? Should I look for a white lady slowly following a scrawny dog, or perhaps, a newer car parked in front of a run-down shack? We did not know, so we looked for all those things. It was fun; it was adventurous, but we were unsuccessful. To be honest, I am glad we did not find the Claw Lady, for like Hal Reichle, I should protect the anonymity of anonymous benefactors.

The Claw Lady wanted to remain anonymous, and because I cannot find anyone who knows who she is, I suggest she has been successful in that endeavor.

How does the Claw Lady pay for her wonderful services? Is she rich and generous? Does she have private funding? Is she part of a government program? If she visits these homes with regularity delivering food, how come no one knows who she is? No one I have found can answer these questions. This is the great benevolent and enchanting mystery of Khayelitsha. These are the things from which legends are made.[118] Another fine example of giving anonymously. Another wonderful hero of peace.

I just had an epiphany; I suspect something wonderful is occurring. I think I unknowingly ran into a clandestine partnership of special heroes. The Claw Lady supplies the orphaned children with food, clothing, and education. What education? The only school for miles was started by and belongs to Glenys van Halter. Are Glenys van Halter and the Claw Lady working together? When Glenys drove me around Khayelitsha looking for the Claw Lady, was this a smokescreen attempting to maintain the Clay Lady's anonymity? Are Glenys and the Claw Lady the same person? Am I allowed to have this much fun?

---

118 This story was told to the author by Glenys van Halter, who lives near Khayelitsha.

THE FLOWER MAN
The Poor Caring for the Poor—Rotary Assisted
City and Country: Khayelitsha, South Africa
Occupation: Artist
Compassionate Endeavor: Supporting starving families

In 2006, a man living in a shack in the township of Khayelitsha, South Africa, was talking to Carol Ruggie outside his lean-to. Carol, a Rotarian on a mission trip from Aurora, Ohio, was interested in helping individuals find employment in South Africa. This was difficult because the unemployment rate was so high. Better success could be obtained if someone started his own business instead of looking for someone to hire him.

Meet the Flower Man
I am going to refer to the man chatting with Carol Ruggie as the Flower Man. He was telling Carol that he was an artist, that he made beautiful flowers from cutting up beer and soda pop cans discarded on the street. He needed $150 to buy paints, brushes, and tools for cutting and forming

the beer cans into sculpted flowers. He could then sell his finished flowers to the public. Carol, not knowing the Flower Man, gave him $150 and wished him well in his planned endeavor.

One year later, in the summer of 2007, Carol Ruggie returned to Khayelitsha, South Africa. I was with her. Carol told me we had to try and locate a special gentleman. We entered Khayelitsha, and based only on Carol's memory, drove around the dirt streets looking for the man to whom Carol had lent $150. We were in luck; Carol's memory prevailed.

We learned he was now called the Flower Man. There was an addition built onto the Flower Man's shack since Carol talked to him the previous year. There was now an artist's workshop strewn with paints, brushes, beer cans rescued from littered streets, and hundreds of completed works of art. The Flower Man took one look at Carol and they both embraced. The Flower Man had a grateful and proud look on his face.

Was the Flower Man Successful?

The Flower Man could hardly contain his excitement as he explained to Carol the story of his success of the past year. He explained that by picking up pop and beer cans from the streets, he has one of the cleanest areas in the township. He further explained that he makes hundreds of daisies, daffodils, and roses from fabricating the cut-up beer cans and then paints these metal works of arts with brilliant colors. But he saved the best part for last. He was giggling so hard he had difficulty talking, and tears were forming and falling from his cheeks.

He proudly exclaimed to Carol that wholesalers buy his flowers by the hundreds, and they pedal them to tourists on the beaches of Cape Town. The Flower Man, with a grin so big I thought his mouth was going to rip, said he is making so much money that he can totally support eight other families with an average of six kids each! He pays for their food, clothing, and medical expenses—anonymously. They do not know who he is.

Carol was now crying too, for her $150 investment and trust in a total stranger had paid off in wonderment. Carol looked around the Flower Man's grass shack. It had no running water and one light bulb hanging on a wire from the thatched roof. Carol inquired, "With all that money, don't you want a better house for yourself?" The Flower Man replied, "If I did that, then two of my eight families would be without food!"

I looked at the remarkable flower configurations and noticed the flower vases were made from the tops of beer cans. Very clever! I bought several roses and have used them as talking aids for over fifty speeches I have given about the Flower Man involving compassion and values. At night, he sleeps well.

Trusting only those who have proven themselves trustworthy
is not trusting at all.
Carol Ruggie

Instead of giving myself reasons why I can't, I give myself reasons why I can.
Anonymous

How many selfish people do you know who are happy?
Unknown

Constant kindness can accomplish much. As the sun makes ice melt, kindness causes misunderstanding, mistrust, and hostility to evaporate.
Albert Schweitzer

Kind words can be short and easy to speak, but their echoes are truly endless.
Mother Teresa

Chapter Five

The Values of Addressing Courage and Perseverance

Addressing Courage

Honor, respect, and welcome fear, for only fear can offer you an opportunity to demonstrate courage.

Perseverance

Never give up. Most perceived failures are not failures at all, but instead successfully completed steppingstones toward a goal. The only time you can fail is if you quit pursuing your goals.

You are the first "you" that ever was. No one can be you as efficiently and effectively as you can. You are the only person with your unique set of abilities, so be yourself; who else is better qualified?
Christopher Morley

The ultimate measure of a man (or woman) is not where he/she stands in moments of comfort and convenience, but where he/she stands at times of challenge and controversy.
Martin Luther King Jr

It is amazing when one person starts a project that later grows into a huge enterprise benefiting millions of people. This often stems from experienced hardships and misfortunes. Such undertakings require a desire to help others avoid or escape the sufferings one has experienced. An example would be a five-year-old street child who grows up to rescue hundreds of street children. Other people grow up watching a mentor show extreme kindness and sacrifice. This kindness is often duplicated in the onlooker's future behavior. A sixteen-year-old girl deciding to rescue hundreds of infants destined for killing in Nazi death camps is an inspiring, even chilling example—but it happened. In this chapter we meet Irena Sendler, Masalakulangwa Mabula, Reverend Corine McClintoc, and Dr. Meena Patel.

IRENA SENDLEROWA (SENDLER)
Rescuing Jewish Infants Under the Nazis' Eyes
Profession: Nurse
Country: Poland
Compassionate endeavor: Rescuing infants and children from
Nazi death camps

In 1939, Germany invaded Poland with the intent to exterminate the Jews. Irena Sendler started helping Jews survive this overwhelming plight by bringing the Jews food and offering them shelter. But in 1940, the Warsaw Ghetto was constructed. The Warsaw Ghetto was a sixteen-block area surrounded by a tall wall and barbed wire—about the size of New York City's Central Park. It would soon confine over 500,000 Jews keeping Irena from contacting them.

Irena's father was a physician devoted to helping those less fortunate. He was the first Polish Socialist. Her father taught her to appreciate and respect others regardless of their ethnicity or social status. Irena later put her life at risk many times because of her father's teachings. He not only preached these values to his daughter but lived by this code as well. He took on many impoverished Jews as patients that other doctors would not see. Irena's father eventually died of Typhus after treating many during the Typhus epidemic in 1917. His last words to his daughter were "If you see someone drowning, you must jump in and try to save them, even if you don't know how to swim." [119]

The ghetto consisted of many apartment buildings filled with Jewish families. All Jews placed in the ghetto were destined for the Nazi death camp at Treblinka, that is unless they died beforehand from disease (often typhoid), starvation, or at the hand of a disgruntled Nazi soldier.

Irena Sendler, to help Jews hide their identity from the Nazis, formed an underground network with her friends working at the Warsaw Social Welfare Department. These helpers, in quiet secrecy, forged over 3,000 identification documents for local Jews.

The Polish underground

Zegota, the name for the Polish underground movement, was trying to save some of the infants in the Warsaw Ghetto before they were transported to Treblinka. Irena was determined to save hundreds of these children, so she joined Zegota to utilize their secretive assets; in fact, she became the head of this risky underground movement. She used the code name "Jolanta" during her secret activities.

At 16 years old, Irena was visiting different apartments in the ghetto disguised as a nurse. Although she was Catholic, she wore a gold Star of David on her clothing to create less suspicion from her presence in the area. She delivered food, clothing, and medicine using a pass she was able to obtain from the Warsaw Epidemic Control Department. She needed to think of secretive ways to smuggle out Jewish children and infants right under the noses of hundreds of Nazi soldiers. She knew, if discovered, that she would be shot. Her first task, however, was to convince the parents to trust her with their babies. Irena earnestly pleaded with them, "I cannot promise that I will be able to save your child, but I can promise that they will be killed at Treblinka if you do not entrust them to me." Irena stated during an interview, "I tried to talk parents out of their children!"

---

119 Early Childhood, Irena Sendler, https://irenasendleressay.weebly.com/early-childhood.html

How can children and infants be smuggled out of the Warsaw Ghetto?

Sometimes Irena placed an infant in a coffin with the body of someone who had recently died. One infant was placed in a carpenter's tool bag. Some were smuggled out in burlap sacks hidden in piles of supplies, others in potato sacks piled with other food stuffs. Sometime a child escaped through the sewer pipes. An ambulance was used when pretending the child was sick. An ambulance was even more successful if the child was sick or was placed on a stretcher or inside a body bag. The courthouse was an abandoned building that was sometimes used as an escape route as well. Sometimes Irena portrayed a plumber fixing broken pipes in the ghetto. Infants were smuggled out inside her plumber's tool satchel. Through these various methods, Irena managed to rescue and place in homes over 2,500 infants. Irena became a major part of this dangerous underground network. Because of her frequent appearances in the Warsaw Ghetto, the Gestapo became suspicious of her activities.

Irena had also recruited into her Zegota underground network her helpers at the Social Welfare Department. Through these clandestine efforts, false identification documents were issued for the children giving them Christian names. Children old enough to talk were taught Christian hymns and prayers and learned how to cross themselves adding a touch of legitimacy to this perilous undertaking.

Irena is arrested and tortured

In hopes of returning some children to their parents after the war, Irena kept a detailed list of each child she smuggled out of the ghetto and where they were placed. She kept this list in a glass jar. It was sad to later discover that almost all the parents of Irena's smuggled children had died in the Treblinka death camp.

On October 20, 1943, because of Irena's suspicious behavior in the Warsaw Ghetto and because of hundreds of missing children, the Nazis became mistrustful and raided her house. Afraid that the list of smuggled children would be discovered, Irena threw the glass jar holding their identities to a friend before she answered the Gestapo pounding on her door. [120]

Pawiak Prison became Irena's new home for the next eight weeks, where she was questioned, tortured, and had her arms and legs broken. She did not betray her smuggled children and told the Gestapo nothing despite the unthinkable torture she endured. She was eventually sentenced to death and given to a Nazi guard who was ordered to take her to the

---

120 *Life in a Jar*, the Irena Sendler Project, http://www.irenasendler.org/facts-about-irena/

woods and shoot her. Zegota spies, however, bribed the guard to simply leave her unattended in the forest to slowly die of her wounds. It was there that she was rescued by her underground comrades and taken to safety. As unbelievable as it sounds, despite her torture and abuse, Irena lived in Poland until she was ninety-eight years old.[121]

Ironically, the glass jar with the names of the 2,500 infants rescued was buried under an apple tree located across the street from Gestapo Headquarters. The Nazis never found it.

Irena stated that she has nightmares every night, not about the horrors of war or the holocaust, but wondering if she had done enough good in her life.[122]

The play and book: "Life in a Jar"

In 1999, four girls attending Union Town High School, located in Uniontown, Kansas, discovered the story of Irena Sendlerowa (Sendler) while researching a story for National History Day. The only mention of Irena was in a 1994 issue of the U.S. News and World Report. Irena's name was listed on only one website.

The discovery of Irena Sendler by these four schoolgirls blew the roof off this wonderful story. In 2001, the girls and their parents visited Poland, not only for additional research, but to visit Irena herself. This trip to Poland, followed by two more later trips, resulted in Irena's story being known to the world. Her name is now listed on well over 500,000 websites.[123]

"Life in a Jar," the play telling the Irena Sendler story, was finished in 1999. It was written by the high school girls of Uniontown, Kansas. It came out as a book in August 2010. It has won nine literary awards.

Irena Sendler was awarded Poland's highest distinction, the Order of White Eagle, in Warsaw on Monday Nov. 10, 2003. In 2008 she was nominated for the Nobel Peace Prize, but Al Gore won the Nobel Prize instead for his work involving global warming. This made me very sad.

You cannot separate others based on race, religion, and creed; you can only separate others on the basis of good and evil.
Irena Sendler

---

121 Ibid
122 *The Irena Sendler Documentary Project,* https://www.youtube.com/watch?v=zHod5W-VDWEA&pbjreload=10
123 Ibid

MASALAKULANGWA MABULA
A Former Street Child Returns to the Streets—Rotary Assisted
Profession: Anglican Priest
Country: Tanzania, Africa
Compassionate endeavor: Rescuing street children

Masalakulangwa (Ma sal la ku lon gwa) was born in Mwanza, Tanzania, Africa. His family was extremely poor. His mother worked as a cleaning lady at a local hospital.

When Masalakulangwa was three years old, his father died. When he was five years old, his mother died. Because there were no other family members able to care for him, he became a street child at the age of five, eating from restaurant's garbage containers, bathing in Lake Victoria, and finding shelter anywhere he could.

To the police, street children were riffraff. They were to be chased away from commercial enterprises because their begging and search for food interfered with the business patrons. They were often beaten with police batons, so they tried to run fast enough to avoid the policeman's assault.

Shortly after Masalakulangwa entered the world of street children, he found it difficult to make friends and trust other street kids. There was a certain protocol on the streets, a specific hierarchy of authority, that had

to be learned, but only from unknowingly violating the protocol and suffering the consequences. Fifteen-year-old kids were much more powerful and controlling than a five-year old like Masalakulangwa. Someone as young as five years old was little more than vulnerable to abuse and easy prey for the demented. It also appeared the police took little notice of a child's age when clearing out an area of "undesirables" with their batons.

Being small, like a five-year-old child, also increased vulnerability to wild dog attacks. Bathing in Lake Victoria also increased dangerous encounters with baboons, snakes, spiders, and even crocodiles. On February 28, 2005, Osama, the crocodile man-eater terror of Lake Victoria, was finishing off a twelve-year-old boy's remains from the Village of Luganga, being the eighty-third victim from that village to succumb to Osama's terror. [124] The homeless in Tanzania have far more dangers to confront than the homeless in New York.

As Masalakulangwa was sitting on a corner diligently watching for other street children, a six-year-old girl, who had just been raped, approached him crying. She was bleeding terribly. Masalakulangwa remembered that his mother used to work at a hospital, and he often visited her there. But would the doctors and nurses remember his mother, or even more critical, would they remember him?

Masalakulangwa, after walking several blocks with the little girl, arrived at the hospital. He was in luck, because both the doctors and nurses remembered him and his mother, and they treated the little girl immediately because of that former relationship. Normally injured or sick street children, the undesirable riffraff who are a nuisance to everyone, are chased away from hospitals.

A new powerful person is on the streets

It is an uncomfortable position for a five-year old child to become king of the street children. But having medical connections that would allow a sick or injured street child to receive medical attention at a hospital was unheard of. All the street children realized what an asset Masalakulangwa was regardless of his young age. After helping the little girl, he was revered, given extra considerations, and was no longer abused by other kids.

How does a child eat while living on the streets?

When restaurants cater birthday parties or special business events, there is frequently lots of leftover food that ends up in the garbage, even if it is only uneaten food scrapped from dinner plates. When found, such garbage creates a feast for the street kids. They stuff themselves as if their next meal were days away, and it might very well be.

Masalakulangwa stayed on the streets until he was twelve years old. His body was heavily scarred from many encounters with police batons and wild dogs roaming the streets competing for food. He was then mirac-

---

124 *The Telegraph*, Osama, terror of Lake Victoria, is caught at last by Adrian Blomfield in Lugamnga, March 13, 2005

ulously taken off the streets by Anglican missionaries. As he was leaving, he promised all the street children that he would be back to help and care for them. He dreamed of helping hundreds of his impoverished friends.[125]

Let's move ahead fifteen years

Masalakulangwa now has a college degree from a university in England as well as another degree from the University of Texas at Austin. He also has a master's degree and has become an Anglican priest and has taught in medical schools. He has returned to the city of Mwanza and, as he promised, is rescuing street children still trying to survive in the brutal back alleys where he reigned as child king for seven years. Masalakulangwa has placed over 250 "Children of High Social Risk" in private homes as he rescues kids from the former life of starvation and brutality that he was exposed to at such an early age. He promised the street children he would do this. He can be trusted.

Hiram College invited Masalakulangwa to the United States for a health conference

In 2006, Hiram College in Hiram, Ohio, was hosting the Global Health-Care Justice Project researching the problems with health services in third-world countries. Masalakulangwa was invited to join the health-care project and give speeches throughout other colleges and community groups in Northeastern Ohio. Masalakulangwa was to live with me in my house in Hiram. I was excited.

The day I met Masalakulangwa, I took him to a grocery store so he could pick out foods he was used to eating in Tanzania. After we went shopping, my refrigerator was filled. The next day, the third day, and the fourth day my refrigerator remained full. He had not eaten anything.

I took him aside and asked if he knew how to use my gas stove. He stated that he did. I told him I noticed he had not eaten any food in the past four days. I inquired if he was eating at the college cafeteria or at another faculty's house? Masalakulangwa stated he has not eaten in four days, that he is so accustomed to living like a street child, that the behavior followed him into his adult life. As a street child, about every three or four days he would come across a feast in a restaurant garbage can. The restaurant had just finished a gala birthday or gradation party and had thrown out uneaten food from many plates. Masalakulangwa would eat his fill but

---

125 From many personal interviews with Masalakulangwa while he was staying at my house in 2007

would probably not find much more food for several days. He lived this way into adulthood.

I asked him if I could take him out to dinner tonight? He excitedly accepted. I had NOT been listening to him, but I was to quickly learn to do so.

That evening Masalakulangwa and I sat down at a moderately expensive restaurant. I wanted him to feel appreciated. I asked him if he wanted an appetizer. He eagerly ordered a shrimp cocktail, followed by a bottle of wine and pork chops for his entrée. When it came time for dessert, my wallet and I were hoping he was full, but we were in great error! For dessert, Masalakulangwa ordered the chicken dinner, and after that, he ordered the fried fish entrée. I just sat there staring at him! He stuffed himself beyond all that was possible. He reminded me that he had not eaten in four days, and that it was time to eat and eat, and repeat the process after not eating for the next few days. Masalakulangwa leaned back in his chair, moaned, loosened his belt, and simply smiled at me. The waiter then brought me the check, and he smiled at me as well.[126]

Masalakulangwa went on to work toward his Ph.D. His thesis topic is Iatrogenia, medical error, and negligence: Divine-Human Creativity Theory and its Contribution Ethics in Medicine." Not bad for a former street kid!

REVEREND CORINE MCCLINTOC
Profession: Manager of Sparrow Village
Country: South Africa
Compassionate endeavor: Children dying of AIDS

The year is 1990. Reverend Corine McClintoc, a 55-year-old Caucasian, lives in Johannesburg, South Africa. She is walking home late at night from a party with friends. A man kneeling in the street and dying from AIDS begged for food as she passed by. Reverend Corine believed, from his emaciated appearance, that he would die in a few days. "You'll not die in the streets while I can do anything about it!" she exclaimed. "Come home with me and die in a bed with some dignity." And take him home

---

126 The author, derived from many personal experiences with Masalakulangwa

she did! Reverend Corine, who lived alone in her house, bathed the stranger, fed him, and put him to bed.

Over the next week, Reverend Corine returned to the streets of Johannesburg and found other men in the same horrible condition. Within seven days, four more emaciated men, all dying from AIDS, occupied other beds in Reverend Corine's home. The purpose of this? "To allow them to die in dignity and not on the streets in the gutter," said Corine.

South Africa was suffering horrible AIDS problems with children

Unemployed mothers living with their many children in tin shanties begged or stole their next meal. Often infants with AIDS were impossible to care for and were abandoned while other children not infected were sold into prostitution so those family members remaining might survive another day. These discarded street children often sought garbage dumps at night depending on the warmth from decay to protect them from the cold.[127] I am not talking about a few unfortunate isolated cases of extreme cruelty that I have chosen to exploit for emphasis. In this world, I speak of millions. I suspect, you may need to come to terms with horrors of this magnitude.

South Africa was extremely poor. Its white Apartheid government did not have enough revenue to care for blacks who were sick and disadvantaged nor any interest in doing so. The government was filled with confusion and unrest as Nelson Mandela was gradually coming to power. They had no money to care for the dying. People dying of AIDS were frequently found abandoned in the streets. Poor families with several children often had to abandon the child with AIDS because the required resources to care for the AIDS child would seriously deplete the money and food needed for the rest of the family. As difficult as it is to imagine, infants with AIDS were often abandoned at night in city garbage dumps. Police officers on patrol would hear their cries, locate them among the garbage, and take them to dying rooms at local hospitals. In these dying rooms, the infants would be ignored until they perished. As I previously stated, there was no money for anyone dying, for there was insufficient resources for the living.[128]

---

127 Ibid
128 This information was obtained from a two-day interview between Roger F. Cram, Carol Ruggie, Reverend Corine, and her staff as we enjoyed meals with her and toured Sparrow Village. 2004

The police heard about Reverend Corine's kindness

One police officer found another infant among the city trash. He had heard about Reverend Corine's kindness to the five men she found dying of AIDS. The police officer did not want to take the baby to the hospital, for he knew the horrible fate that awaited the child at such facilities. This police officer wondered if Reverend Corine would be willing to care for this infant as she was caring for the five men? He took the infant to Reverend Corine's house. The infant was, of course, eagerly accepted.

The word about Reverend's Corine's kindness spread quickly throughout the police department. Within one week, there were so many infants in so many cribs in Reverend Corine's kitchen that she could not open her refrigerator. Within three more weeks, there were so many infants in so many cribs in the kitchens of Reverend Corine's neighbors that none of them could open their refrigerators!

It became obvious that Reverend Corine had a major problem on her hands. She decided to build a village for children dying of AIDS and allow their parents to stay with them, something usually not allowed at similar facilities. She would call it Sparrow Village after the reference to sparrows in the Christian Bible—"His eye is on the sparrow, and I know he is watching over me" (Matthew 6:26).

When Reverend Corine applied for a permit to build a clinic for children dying of AIDS, the government denied her request stating that she was not a qualified doctor. Not giving up, Reverend Corine applied for a permit to build a school but was turned down again because she was not a certified teacher and did not meet the requirements of an approved school. Being persistent, she applied for permission to build a hospice for dying children. She was informed that no permit was needed to start a hospice. Reverend Corine did not mention that her hospice was going to have a clinic and a school.

But how does one go about building a village with little funds? Building costs were expensive. A friend of Reverend Corinne told her that he had a huge balloon with a thirty-foot diameter. He suggested that she blow up the balloon until it became a thirty-foot sphere, then cover it in bricks allowing room for windows and doorways. Then let the air out, remove the balloon through the door, and blow it up again and build another igloo-shaped structure.[129]

Pictured on the facing page is a huge balloon being covered with bricks by homeless men recently trained in brick masonry. When this igloo-type

---

129 Ibid

structure was finished, they covered it in plaster, painted it, and moved on to start the next structure.

Caring for the homeless

Reverend Corine loved the balloon-igloo idea. She asked several professional carpenters, brick masons, and electricians to volunteer their time training homeless men in those occupational skills. Then the homeless could build her village and maintain it. Such a plan worked marvelously! The finished igloo is nothing short of charming, almost enchanting, and the thought of an entire village of these little-domed huts conjure up visions of something one might imagine in a dream.

The mission statement of Sparrow Village

Reverend Corine McClintock, to raise money for the development of Sparrow Village, printed a general history-type document informing others of her plan. That highly informative document was sent to those seeking information about Sparrow Village. An excerpt is printed below.

Dear Friends of Sparrow Village:

Our sole purpose is to alleviate the pain and suffering of destitute terminally ill adults and children with AIDS.

We started the Hospice in 1992 with 4 patients.

The first three patients were men. They were young, in their late 20's, homosexual, and suffering from a relatively 'new' disease. Their relatives could not cope, and mostly, left them at provincial hospitals, who in turn needed to discharge them. Nowhere to go, they were left on the streets to die alone, without anyone to care for them. Obviously, over the years this problem escalated, including over 40% of children....

As apartheid was still present in South Africa, we very quietly called the hospice a "Guesthouse," and the patients, our "Guests."

In South Africa, the face of AIDS changed from White, homosexual men to heterosexual White and African individuals.

We are currently looking after adults and children. All destitute and terminally ill. Our patients are mostly mothers between the ages of 19–35 with young babies.

Another lesson learned over the years was not to separate mother and child, since the mother would often feel guilty having her meals, while her baby was possibly starving. She also had the added guilt that she had infected her child with HIV.

We also realized that the bond between mother and child should not be severed prematurely, and we watched many mothers with their children that stay with us, thrive for this reason.

Since opening, we have lost over 600 patients at this hospice. To remember all of them, we started putting little metal 'sparrows' on a tree of remembrance with their names, date of birth—and death.

One patient, very poignantly said that his relatives have deserted him, he felt that he had done 'horrible' things in his life, and because of that no one would want to remember him.

We were able to tell him, that he will not be forgotten, and his story will live on.

We are in the process of compiling a 'Book of Memories' to this effect.

Sparrow Ministries offer a comprehensive medical, psychological, social and spiritual care service through a multi-disciplinary team of qualified personnel offering their expertise mostly on a pro bono basis. We primarily function as an in-patient Hospice facility and have an extensive network of trained Home-Based Care caregivers who care for outpatients in their homes, as our hospice accommodation facility is limited.

It is generally felt that someone with a terminal illness like AIDS should rather be cared for in the familiar surroundings of their own homes by their loved ones. However, listed below are our experiences with regard to this, and also is it not passing the buck to save on bed space and costs for long term chronic care?

 (a) AIDS patients are victimized and ostracized, 'thrown out' by a fearful community.

 (b) Adult relatives are breadwinners and need to work to support the rest of the family.

(c) Relatives have little access to further medical assistance and insubstantial medical expertise—we can tell frightening stories of how dying patients starved to death because relatives did not know how to make them swallow fluids.

 (d) Patients sometimes live in a one-room shack with small children, posing a health hazard to these children when they have TB, diarrhea etc.

 (e) Relatives are not able to cope with the emotional burden of caring for their mother, father or child, not to mention heavy terminal nursing care.

(f) Relatives are ignorant of the stages of HIV/AIDS and care for a son or daughter for up to 6 years whilst still in the HIV "well stage." When this person enters the 'full-blown' AIDS stage, they are psychologically, socially and financially drained and are unable to cope. These outpatients should be accommodated in our hospice, with the destitute and terminally ill.

A 6.4 ha[130] property has finally been awarded to us and we are building a 200-bed hospice that will include a massive children's village. The number of abandoned HIV+, terminally ill babies and children is increasing daily and we have at least 60 babies on our waiting list. Only 40% of our children lost their mothers at Sparrow's. The remainder, have been abandoned at local maternity wards, and in other instances, in dustbins....

We recently had to make space for a mother and her 3 children, whom she had tied to herself to prevent them from wondering off, as she was too weak to supervise them. This family hadn't had anything to eat, as far as we could tell, for over 3 days.

Not to leave you with a lingering feeling of sadness, we have included beautiful, hopeful photographs of some of our children that we currently look after. I am sure that their lives will inspire you as they have inspired us.

Kind regards
Rev. Corine McClintock [131]

I remember Carol Ruggie trying to get a Rotary International grant for human-refrigeration units to serve as a morgue for all the children dying at Sparrow Village. Nine months later, just before the grant was approved, the refrigeration units were no longer needed because of the excellent care given the children from Reverend Corine and her loving staff. Few children were now dying.

---

130 Ha is the abbreviation for hectare, being a metric unit of square with 100-meter sides or 10,000 square meters.
131 This document was an email from Reverend Corine McClintock to Carol Ruggie. This was given to me by Carol Ruggie before she died from pancreatic cancer. I visited Sparrow Village with Carol Ruggie and interviewed Reverend Corine over a period of two days in 2004.

A true success story

The AIDS children were surviving. A fully staffed pharmacy and medical clinic was part of Sparrow Village. Three vans were provided by the City of Johannesburg so Reverend Corine's staff could go into the city and service destitute youth suffering from AIDS. That was wonderful, for it originally was the City of Johannesburg that refused permits for a clinic and a school discouraging Reverend Corine from starting her facility. Now the City is a major supporter.

Reverend Corine informed me that they had provided care for over 10,000 children living outside their facility in the surrounding Johannesburg area. Some of the original children in Sparrow Village were now teenagers. Reverend Corine discussed with me her plans to build a large separate dormitory for these older children addressing their special needs. The annual Sparrow Village budget was over $1 million. What a success story.

When I visited Sparrow Village in 2004 and 2006, there were over 200 children receiving love and care at the enchanted facility. Carol Ruggie had died from pancreatic cancer. During my 2006 visit, I spread one half of Carol Ruggie's ashes throughout Sparrow Village accompanied by prayers and visions of hope for these beautiful children of AIDS. I spread the other half of Carol's ashes at the Children of the Dump School in Chinandega, Nicaragua (See the upcoming hero Frank Huezo).

Other humanitarian causes adopt the Sparrow-Village concept

The Sparrow-Village concept of building a village by training the homeless in the skills of construction had taken hold. Sparrow Village had become famous, and over fifty-four villages in thirty countries had been constructed following the Sparrow-Village model.[132]

One 55-year-old woman with a vision can accomplish much.

If you can't feed one hundred people, then just feed one.
Mother Teresa

---

132 Reported to the author in a personal interview by Reverend Corine in 2006, South Africa

DR. MEENA PATEL
The Angel of Problem Solving—Rotary Assisted
Profession: Doctor and surgeon—ears, nose, and throat
Country: U.S.A. and India
Compassionate endeavor: education, employment, women's rights,
medical services for the poor

*All progress is precarious, and the solution of one problem brings us
face to face with another problem.*
Dr. Martin Luther King Jr.

Dr. Meena Patel has what I call a "serendipitous knack" for problem solving. This ability is quite mysterious and wonderful at the same time. First, she sees a great need and then resolves it, but in doing so creates another need requiring equal attention. Many of these problems are addressed through the world network of Rotary Clubs as described under my hero of peace, Paul Harris.

Dr. Meena Patel, an ear, nose, and throat surgeon in Dover, Ohio, has a knack of making everyone's Rotary dreams come true. Being originally from India, Dr. Patel frequently visits her homeland helping Rotary clubs

care for the destitute. Many of the ghettos in India are as depicted in the movie *Slumdog Millionaire*. Women usually do not go to school, are often treated without dignity, and can be forced into marriage by the age of thirteen.

In India, wives are usually subservient to their husbands. They spend a great deal of time walking miles each day gathering firewood to cook their husband's meals. Frequently, a wife cooks a hot lunch at home for her husband and then delivers it at noon to his place of employment. Because of all these family obligations, women have little time to go to school.

Dr. Meena Patel saw the great need for educating women in India. Gathering supporters and raising funds for a woman's school would accomplish little if some husbands would not allow their wives to attend. The time required to gather firewood, cook a hot lunch, and deliver it to their husbands prohibited attending school. Could the success of a new educational enterprise for women be partially based on some husbands receiving lunch every day? Dr. Meena Patel saw this obstacle and understood its importance within the Indian culture.

A new invention for cooking lunches was required

One thing India has no shortage of is hot sunshine. Dr. Meena Patel discovered an aluminum lunch box containing several aluminum water-tight containers. Uncooked soups, vegetables, meats, and sauces will cook from the solar heat within a few hours if this aluminum lunch box is left out in the sun. A husband now takes his solar-cooking lunch box to work, places it outside in the sun, and has a hot and fully cooked lunch when needed. The wife now has time for school. Problem solved.

Working around the Indian culture

Some men in her area of the world see no need to educate women in the disciplines of language, art, mathematics, computer science, and physics. They believe a woman's job is to raise children, clean the house, cook the meals, and care for the livestock. Many husbands would question the benefits of their wives studying such non-pertinent subjects when time was needed for them to provide a home for their spouse and family.

Dr. Meena Patel realized the importance of domestic chores contributing to the unity of a marriage and family. Therefore, her schools took great pride in teaching culinary arts, not just cooking. Everyday dinners would often become gourmet treats to remember, filled with nutrition, not just routine meals. By taking classes on the economics of proper livestock management, the women were able to provide healthier livestock and cleaner surroundings which resulted in more future revenue from their livestock sales. After women took classes on psychology and adolescent health, their children were better adjusted, calmer, had richer relationships with both parents, and were better prepared to be successful in the future. Attending classes involving sewing and embroidery, women were able to make higher quality clothes for their families. Husbands and fathers rarely complained about receiving such advantages from their wives and daughters attending school. Of course, in addition to the above domestic subjects, the school also taught language, physics, mathematics, art, and music.

Interwoven financial enterprises

If women are going to attend classes in mathematics, economics, and physics, it could be assumed that there will be opportunities for future employment, business start-ups, or other future financial gain. In fact, the school is structured for such outcomes. Dr. Patel arranged, through Rotary Clubs, to furnish the schools with 160 sewing machines and the needed instruction for their use. Through sewing and other crafts, the women supply their school store with purses, jewelry, clothing, and other items for sale. The revenue from sales not only is used to support the school, but the girls attending school are each given 10 rupees per sale to help compensate them for their labor. This money is held in trust until they graduate. By then it has grown to about 40,000 rupees or around $1,000. The money is given to them upon graduation to help start a business.

Guess what one of the businesses is that has been generated by mothers attending the school? If you guessed child care, you are correct. Women taking child care classes often have young children at home. Creating child care services for the mothers attending school provides a necessary service.

Also working with Rotary Clubs, Dr. Patel arranged through banks, microfinance loans to start businesses for many of these woman. Over 18,000 women have received microloans for their self-employment. The day care centers previously mentioned were started from these microloans.

In summation of Dr. Patel's accomplishments, she answered the critical need for educating women by building a quality school. In the process, she supplied hot lunches for working husbands, improved the quality of home meals, enhanced home livestock management, enriched adolescence and family life, and established a store for student products. This enterprise provided money for the students upon graduation. Dr. Patel was also instrumental in arranging thousands of microloans for women to start local business.

The medical needs of the Indian poor

Worldwide, close to 30,000 children five years of age and younger die each day from poor drinking water or not having any water at all. The quality of drinking water in Indian village homes is often deplorable. The women attending the schools started by Dr. Patel frequently have polluted water at their homes as well as at their school.

Through Dr. Patel's influence and guidance, water wells have been installed in over fifty remote Indian villages. This wonderful solution to poor water quality created another problem that had to be addressed. These fifty water wells often lowered the underground water table to dangerously low levels. Therefore, Dr. Patel started a water retention project so more of the monsoon rains would be sent underground. She arranged for the installation of rooftop water systems sending the rains to the underground through a series of roof gutters, storage tanks, and open drains. This kept much the rain from flowing away, kept the underground water table adequate, and allowed some water wells to be used for crop irrigation as well.

Now the children had clean drinking water at home, but they had to drink unhealthy water at their schools. Dr. Patel then persuaded local Rotary clubs to install water filters at schools. Now having clean water at home and school at many Indian villages, everyone's health has been greatly improved.

Dr. Patel then went to work providing medical operations in several Indian villages. Many polio corrective surgeries were made possible by her never-ending efforts. Working with local Rotary Clubs, she became instrumental in over 1,500 myopia and cataract eye operations. By her financing modern laser surgery equipment for clinics, hundreds of poor Indians, many who have not been able to see for over forty years, now enjoy the gift of sight.

Furnished through the Rotary Clubs in Japan, there is now an eye-surgery van equipped with laser surgery and lens replacement techniques that visits remote villages in India. Other funding has provided another medical bus for general practitioner doctors caring for thousands of the Indian poor.

One woman, with the heart of a saint enshrouded by insatiable determination, has greatly enriched the lives of thousands. When I talk with her and discuss her humanitarian projects, I am confronted with a soft-spoken, unassuming woman who considers herself privileged to be able to serve others—a true hero of peace to herself and others.

During September 2022, I talked with Dr. Meena Patel over the phone while she was in India assisting the poor. I asked her how she feels about her remarkable successes serving the poor and her new projects she is currently involved with. She sent me the following email:

It has been a humbling experience to see the sustainability of the projects undertaken during last 20 years and their measurable desired results in improving the life of the beneficiaries. I continue to work with the Rotarians in India, (and occasionally in Kenya), where I do most of my work, as I travel to that country every year spending 3-4 months, giving myself the opportunity to visit the project sites and meet the beneficiaries appreciating their expressed gratitude to the Rotarians for making the difference!

If any project does not get desired results, (happens in about 5–10% projects in spite of good evaluation of the needs and proper planning), it gives me the opportunity to evaluate and get the insight into what else could be done to improve the outcome.

I have concentrated on adopting a community or adopting the vocations like farming, healthcare, or sometimes combine more than one focus area that would give better results. eg:

1. Providing water to each home in a village, making life of women easy before establishing a goat farm for them and then encouraging women and men to develop other supporting vocations.

2. Small land-holding farmers in many villages of India who are unable to sustain their livelihood by farming because of increased cost of machinery and tools, fertilizers, pesticides and weed killers. A large number of these farmers are committing suicide, as they are unable to sustain the family expenses. At present, the work is going on to change the mind of the farmers, the believes that are millennia old, and use new well tested methods like No-Till technique, using cover crops, and keeping the earthworms undisturbed in the soil.

3. Home health care was not available in India for the majority of the population that is poor. My Rotary partners established the first of its kind The Home Health Care Equipment Center on a smaller scale when Covid-19 devastation hit poor Indian population disproportionately.

—The Rotary Foundation's good work is continued on!!!

It is not possible to be in favor of justice for some people and not be in favor of justice for all people.
Martin Luther King, Jr.

Only a life lived in the service to others is worth living.
Albert Einstein

If you want to lift yourself up, lift up someone else.
Booker T. Washington

All that is necessary for the triumph of evil is that good people do nothing.
Edmund Burke

I always tell my volunteers that you are the change that you dream, and I am the change that I dream. And collectively we are the change that this world needs to be.
Efren Penaflorida

Chapter Six

The Values of Encouraging Trust and Managing Conflict

Encouraging Trust

Honor all commitments and obligations to everyone, especially yourself. Your pledge should be as meaningful to a king as to a beggar, for the value of a commitment is determined from its source, not to whom it is directed.

Managing Conflict

While engaging your adversaries, always maintain their dignity. This is the only road to lasting peace.

Preserving Character

How you react to any incident not only determines your true character, but boldly announces to all onlookers who you are. Therefore, courageously fulfill the obligations of being human by revering all life, defending the righteous, promoting peace, spreading compassion, rendering joy, and sharing your assets* with those less fortunate.

Revering these Values

Uphold this Value System, especially under adverse conditions, not to please someone else, but to honor the unfaltering principles within you, to validate your character as the type of person you want to be, and to gradually realize the awesome potential of being human.

Always aim for the moon; if you miss, you'll end up in the stars.
(Tuskegee Airmen Youth Group—Gaylord TX, Tuskegee Airmen
Convention—August 21, 2007)

You cannot prepare for peace and war at the same time.
Albert Einstein

When the whole world is silent, even one voice becomes powerful.
Malala Yousafzai

Having a vision or a dream about a future project or goal is something only humans can do. The Empire State Building was once a vision in someone's mind, as was the Great Wall of China, as was landing a man on the moon. Dr. Jonas Salk, a doctor in South Africa, had a vision of finding a cure for polio.[133] Nelson Mandela, who was imprisoned for 27 years, had a vision of bringing peace to South Africa and became its first black president.[134] How did *vision, perseverance,* and *values* help these great heroes reach their goals?

Ginetta Sagan was four feet eleven inches tall as she boldly confronted the dictators of many tortuous regimes, and Mother Teresa, barely five feet tall, spent a life caring for the dying among the lepers in the infested back alleys of Calcutta.

If I do not have the opportunity to run toward the frontlines of today's misfortunes, I can become involved with the logistics needed for their defeat. Without the organizers, the fund raisers, the promoters, the speech makers, and the "grunt" workers, those on the front lines would surely fail. One position is not more important than the other; they are all critical links in the chain of human caring. A multi-million dollar undertaking to feed the impoverished in Bangladesh has hundreds of links and thousands of workers along its project implementation chain. However, this magnificent project might fail if a twelve-year old volunteer fails to put postage stamps on the promotional material. Everyone is critically important. In this final chapter, I introduce Gilbert Doho, Olga Sanchez, John Robert Lewis, and the team of Father Marco Dessy and Frank Huezo.

GILBERT DOHO
Fights for Women's Rights by Stealth and Incognito
Country: Cameroon, Africa
Profession: Politician, educator
Compassionate Endeavor: Woman's rights through theater

The introduction of this book starts with a quote from Gilbert Doho: "If what you did during your last hour only benefited you, you should not have done it. If what you plan to do during your next hour only benefits you, don't do it!"

---

133 *This Day in History*, March 25, 1953, www.history.com
134 *BBC News*, by Mike Wooldridge, December 11, 2013, *How he Survived 27 Years in Prison*

Such a remarkable and inspiring quote could only come from a remarkable and inspiring person.

Gilbert Doho is an associate French professor at the prestigious Case Western Reserve University in Cleveland, Ohio. Part of his education was financed by his mother, who picked coffee beans in Cameroon, Africa, for sixty years. She also made a special bread from a type of root growing along

some roadways in Cameroon. This bread was then sold to passersby from her little roadside stand.

Once Gilbert had obtained his degrees and was successful, he purchased a house in Cameroon. His mother visited Gilbert in his home and was served a strange brown hot liquid. Gilbert's mother inquired what it was? Can you imagine picking coffee beans for sixty years and not knowing what happens to them? Gilbert's mother had no idea that the hot brown liquid she was served, coffee, was the final product created from the beans she had picked all her adult life. Most of the coffee plantations were owned by the Cameroon government. The poor were exploited for manual labor. They simply picked the beans and put them into a large burlap sack. When it was filled, they repeated the process.

Cameroon and Human Rights

Women's rights in Cameroon were limited in the 1950s and 1960s and still today. When a husband died, the widow was forced to marry her husband's brother. Education was limited for females. Marital rape was not a criminal offense.[135] To prevent early teen pregnancies and thus disgracing the family, FGC (Female Genital Cutting) is practiced. In such a circumstance, the external female genitals are cut off and then the vagina is sewed shut with thorns. No anesthetic is used, and the girl, held down by community members during the gruesome process, often bleeds to death or dies from

---

135 Wiki Gender, Africa for Women's Rights: Cameroon, https://www.wikigender.org/wiki/africa-for-womens-rights-cameroon/

infections. [136] One girl suffers FGC somewhere in the world every ten seconds. [137] This cruelty exists to stop a girl from having premarital sex or to prevent her from enjoying it.

Breast ironing is another deterrent to keep developing girls from physically tempting men. In Cameroon and other backward countries, many men feel a girl is available for sex when her breasts develop. Breast ironing is the use of a heated object or hard pestle used to pound or flatten the developing breasts of a young girl.[138]

Fighting for Women's rights through theater

Gilbert Doho traveled around Cameroon as a common citizen. He entered a small village and stayed for several months. He assisted them with their community responsibilities and made many lasting friendships. His real reason for being in the village is to increase awareness of how poorly women are treated. However, had he started giving speeches about the lack of women's rights practiced there, he would have been kicked out of the village or arrested. To avoid arrest, he pretended to be a visitor interested in getting to know the villagers, while in reality his purpose was to increase awareness of discrimination against women. Gilbert maintained this stealth, incognito, for several months.

Eventually, after establishing the community's trust, he started some poetry readings. This was greatly appreciated and welcomed by all. He then encouraged others to publicly read poetry and tell stories in community gatherings. Admiration, appreciation, and trust of him were ever growing among the villagers.

As the weeks passed, Gilbert introduced the thought of putting on a community play with all the actors being from the village. They would create a performance for themselves to entertain and educate each other. A script must be written for each part in the play. A stage must be created as well as scenery and props. But what would the play be about? What subject matter should be addressed?

Gilbert held brainstorming sessions for days as the villagers tried to decide between comedy or drama, a heavy theme or a lighthearted one. Gilbert was indirectly guiding the villager's ideas toward something important, toward a cause, toward a right or wrong, or an evolving tribal custom or belief. When the villagers selected a theme for their play, through Gilbert's skillful guidance, they believe they had chosen the subject matter

---

136 Tostan, *Dignity for All*, Molly Melching, http://skoll.org/organization/tostan/
137 *Half the Sky*, Chapter 13, Nicholas D. Kristof, authors and columnist for New York Times,
138 Ibid

themselves. Gilbert, despite his multiple inputs, in the minds of the villagers, was able to remain a bystander.

The play might be a comedy about a rebellious wife demanding things that women are not entitled to. Her obnoxious requests for equality in the marriage would be presented as a satirical farce creating laughter from the audience.

As the audience watches the play, they often get a refreshing perspective by observing the female lead suffer inequalities compared to the males. Gilbert told me that after the performance, villagers often think for several days about a change in their customs that offers closer equality. The ladies would not be allowed to openly criticize a tribal custom without retaliation, but openly exposing some unjust customs to everyone through a community play creates great food-for-thought and a new awareness. This sometimes results in a second play addressing a woman's rights issue more directly. Gilbert remains a tribal friend; the villagers give themselves credit for their realizations into women's rights. Soon Gilbert Doho leaves the village moving on to another little community. He starts the process over again. Ego-free compassion at its finest! Giving without recognition.

Fighting for women's human rights in Cameroon is difficult

Gilbert Doho was invited to the King's palace in Cameroon for dinner. As he entered the palace, he noticed the king seated on his throne and his many wives sprawled out on the floor beneath him. Gilbert Doho also noticed a nice sitting area next to the king's throne designed for his honored guests. However, being a spirited human-rights advocate, Gilbert Doho sat on the floor in front of the king with his many wives. The king seemed displeased and, in a stern voice addressed Gilbert.

"Are you trying to insult me in my own home!?"

Gilbert responded in a kind voice, "No, your majesty, not at all. I am trying to honor your wives."

The king responded, "That tactic might work in South Africa, but it will not work in Cameroon."

And with that pronouncement, Gilbert Doho was escorted out of Cameroon. That's right, he was kicked out the country for trying to respect women.

Closing thought on Gilbert Doho

Completing great accomplishments anonymously requires skill and planning. It is also conducive to special circumstances where the identity of the benefactor would prevent success of the project. One example would be Gilbert Doho's chosen methodology developed to fight for women's rights. Had Gilbert entered a village pointing out the unfairness and inequities of their customs regarding women, he would have been driven out of the village. By being clever enough for the villagers to think the theme for their upcoming play was their idea, Gilbert accomplishes his mission while remaining safe.

OLGA SANCHEZ
Rescues Victims of the Beast—Rotary Assisted
Profession: Medical clinic owner and operator
City and Country: Tapashula, Mexico
Compassionate endeavor: Rescuing injured migrants

The next time you criticize illegal immigrants sneaking across the United States/Mexican border, please pause for one moment to consider "why" they are doing so. Most of them are fleeing for their lives from starvation, the murderous Mexican drug cartels, and suppression that could easily result in death. Over 50% are women and children, and as of 2014, over half are from Central America, not Mexico. How do they travel the 1,200-mile journey through Mexico to the United States?

The Train of Death
A freight train leaves Arriaga in Chiapas, Mexico, heading northbound for the United States on railroad tracks that are insufficiently maintained. The maintenance of the tracks is so poor that there is at least one derailment each month sending boxcars and tanker cars tumbling into forests and rocky deserts. The greater problem, on top of these box cars are hundreds of people fleeing for their lives.

This train is called, "The Beast." It is also called the "Train of Death." Thousands of poor migrants from Mexico, Guatemala, Honduras, El Salvador, and Nicaragua ride "the Beast" on top of the box cars and tanker cars as they perilously seek a better life in the United States.

These desperate people must stay awake for days hanging on to their small space on the train. If they fall asleep, they fall off the train and get sucked under the wheels losing arms, legs, and often their lives. Over 500 immigrants lose their life annually on the "Beast" trying to find a better life.

Photographs of this event are unbelievable. Go out to the Internet searching for "The Train of Death" or "The Beast." You will not believe what you are seeing!

Criminals are waiting to rob, rape, and kill migrants when the train stops

When the Beast stops, these vulnerable people are robbed, raped, and killed by gangs and corrupt police waiting for them. Many are kidnapped and later found dead. Some migrants have families back home wire what money they have to Western Union stations along the route. In this way they won't be carrying money which attracts attention from criminals.

There are many criminals riding the Beast impersonating migrants. They get to know the migrants, who has money, and who is hiding valuables, so they can be robbed at the next stop.

In 2011, seventy migrants were killed in one incident by these ruthless gangs. Hundreds are raped. Although thousands ride the "Beast" each year, less than 20% successfully make it to the United States. Hundreds fall from the train, severing their arms and legs.

In 1990, Olga Sanchez was in a hospital getting treatment for an intestinal issue. According to an interview Sanchez gave to the Christian Science Monitor, Sanchez, while in the hospital, "met a couple from El Salvador that had fallen off a train in their attempt to get to the US: one had lost an arm, the other a leg." Olga found a soft spot in her heart for the plight of these migrants, and she invited them to come to her home so she could nurse them back to health by healing their wounds and spirits. Shortly afterwards, Olga met more migrants that had lost limbs from falling off the Beast. Olga started scouring hospitals looking for more amputees. She found many and brought them all to her home. She had started her life's work; she had found that special meaning that so many of us are looking for. "I focused on migrants because they were all alone," Olga said, "but they also give back to me, they give me the courage to face my own health problems." [139]

Known as the Mother Teresa of Mexico, Olga Sanchez started to walk the train tracks in 1990. She rescued those who have fallen from the train and picked up their severed arms and legs. She has been running a hostel to care for mutilated migrants in the city of Tapachula, Mexico, ever since.

---

139 By Sara Miller Llana, Staff writer of The Christian Science Monitor July 31, 2007, https://www.csmonitor.com/2007/0731/p07s02-woam.html

Olga states she has tended to thousands of men and women who have lost their legs and arms from riding the Beast.[140]

Food, shelter, medical care, and education are provided

Olga houses her rescued migrants, she feeds them, and she provides schooling and medical care. She wants each one to leave her hospital with prosthetic limbs which cost $2,000–$4,000 each. Olga goes begging door-to-door to raise this money in addition to selling cakes that she bakes at the clinic. "She has received some international donations but raises the extra cash she needs to provide migrants with prosthetic legs by selling bags of home-baked bread for $2 per loaf."[141]

Olga is rescuing so many people, that in 2005 she had to build a new hostel, for her modest home was hopelessly overcrowded. Her home is filled with crutches and wheelchairs. Doctors come to operate on those who have fallen prey to the Beast.[142]

"Since 1990, I've seen more than 8,000 amputees. I used to pick them up from the tracks. I picked up their bones and their remains, people who were almost dead."

"I remember the first one. His name was Baltazar. I picked his bones up from the track. He was dying, clinging to life by a thread. I said to him, 'Remember you have a wife and children; remember, you have to go home. Fight for your family!' I was carrying his bones in my blouse. I was all bloodied."[143]

In 2004, Olga Sanchez received Mexico's National Prize for Human Rights. I am sorry to report that Olga Sanchez, 76, of Uvalde, Mexico, died on Feb. 27, 2018, while living in San Antonio.[144]

---

140 Train to U.S. Spits out Mutilated Migrants by Karl Penhaul, CNN, June 25, 2010, http://www.cnn.com/2010/WORLD/americas/06/24/mexico.amputees/index.html
141 Ibid
142 By Sara Miller Llana, Staff writer of The Christian Science Monitor July 31, 2007, https://www.csmonitor.com/2007/0731/p07s02-woam.html
143 Ibid
144 Uvalde Leader News, March 1, 2018, Olga Sanchez

JOHN ROBERT LEWIS
Utilizes Courage Beyond One's Comprehension
Born on July 17, 1940, as a sharecropper's son in Alabama.
Died July 17, 2020
Profession: Congressman
Country: United States
Compassionate endeavor: Civil rights, equality, equal opportunity.

On rare occasions, heroes arise who believe so strongly in their convictions that they repeatedly subject themselves to violence and injury while fighting for the rights and dignity of others. John Robert Lewis was such a hero.

When Lewis was four years old in Troy, Alabama, he was visiting his Aunt Seneva with thirteen other children—all his cousins. Aunt Seneva's house was a cabin with a wooden floor, but without a foundation. A tornado formed close to the house and the severe winds were trying to lift a corner of the cabin. All the children held hands and walked over to the rising corner so their combined weight would help hold the house down. Then the wind started to lift another corner of the cabin, so all the children walked over to that corner trying to keep it on the ground. They were walking with the wind trying to save the cabin and possibly their livers.[145] This endeavor continued several times until the tornado passed. *Walking with the Wind* was to be the name of John Lewis's book serving as his memoirs. It was completed in 1998.

John Lewis, when he was about seven years old, asked his parents why there were "White Only" and "Colored Only" signs on drinking fountains and rest rooms throughout the south. His parents stated, "That's the way it is. Don't get in the way. Don't get in trouble."[146] Lewis may not have understood this advice, for shortly afterwards he tried to desegregate his school. He knew the difference between getting into trouble and getting into "good trouble." Lewis addressed an audience in 2013 talking about his efforts fighting segregation. Lewis stated, "I got in the way. I got in trouble. Good trouble."[147] The term "good trouble" stayed with him as a motto to influence many.

145 *Walking with the Wind, A Memoir of the Movement*, John Lewis, Simon and Schuster, New York, 1998
146 *The Boston Globe*, "The Conscious of the Congress, the Conscious of America." By Renee Graham, July 18, 2020.
147 Ibid

In 1960, John attended college in Nashville and studied philosophy, the philosophy of non-violence, the philosophy of how to love those abusing you. Apparently, Nashville was a good place to study such civilized endeavors, for Nashville was the first city in the United States to allow whites and blacks to eat together in restaurants.[148]

Lewis was so highly inspired by the civil rights efforts of Dr. Martin Luther King Jr. and Rosa Parks, that he, as a teenager, started fighting for human rights. In 1961, Lewis joined "Freedom Rides" at southern bus stations and "sit-ins" at segregated lunch counters to help reduce and bring awareness to the inhumane segregation and prejudicial treatment of black citizens. This resulted in his arrest, the first of over forty arrests yet to come, and almost as many future assaults by police officers. In 1963, Lewis, participated in planning this country's notable March on Washington D.C. This activity was instrumental in him becoming one of the nation's top six civil-rights leaders.[149]

John Robert Lewis was one of the original thirteen Freedom Riders. I remember the "Freedom Rides" in 1961 when Freedom Riders rode Trailways and Greyhound Buses throughout the southern states This was in bold compliance with the new 1960 Supreme Court ruling (Boynton v. Virginia) stating that segregation on public bus transportation was unconstitutional. At seventeen years old, I watched on the television news as passengers were beaten when they got off buses after arriving at various destinations throughout the south. I did not understand where they got the courage to be Freedom Riders knowing they would probably be severely assaulted when they arrived at their destinations. I did not understand if the Supreme Court ruled it was legal for blacks to ride on interstate buses, why were they being assaulted when they rode on these buses and arrived at their destinations? I was learning about hate. I was learning about courage.

On May 14, 1961, a Greyhound Bus was set on fire in Anniston, Alabama. Ku Klux Klan members attacked the Freedom Riders with baseball bats after their bus arrived in Birmingham severely beating black and white supporters. On May 20, 1961, a horde of whites armed with baseball bats and lead pipes met a bus arriving in Montgomery from Birmingham and attacked the disembarking passengers severely injuring many. Nearby black citizens witnessing the attack intervened rescuing the Freedom

148 "Good Trouble" video about John Robert Lewis, Nongola Pictures, AGC and TIME Studios, CNN Films 2020
149 John Lewis, Biography, Accomplishments, and Facts / Britannica.com / Wallenfeldt, Jeff, Editor, Encyclopedia Britannica, August 3, 2020

Riders from further assault. It was time for righteous citizens to take matters into their own hands.

When you see something that is not right, is not fair, not just, you have to speak up. You have to say something. You have to do something.
John Robert Lewis

Nonviolent activists organized a peaceful 54-mile walk from Selma, Alabama to the capital Montgomery. On February 18. 1965, a peaceful demonstration encouraging equal voting rights for blacks was taking place in Marion, Alabama. Jimmie Lee Jackson, a twenty-seven-year-old civil rights activist and deacon of the local Baptist Church, noticed his mother, who was marching in the demonstration, being attacked by a state trooper with a Billy club. Jackson rushed to cover his mother with his body trying to protect her from the trooper's blows. He was shot for doing so and died seven days later.

On March 7, 1965, civil rights leaders, fighting for equality at the voting booth for blacks, were about to make history in Selma, Alabama. John Robert Lewis, at twenty-five-years-of-age, led 600 civil rights protesters over the Edmund Pettus Bridge in Selma. Dr. Martin Luther King Jr. was marching in this demonstration along with other top civil-rights leaders. They were all following John Lewis. Waiting for the peaceful demonstrators on the other side of the bridge were county sheriff deputies, some on horseback; city police, state troopers, and sworn-in citizen militia all armed with Billy clubs. Many white spectators waving confederate flags were eager to see the upcoming violence.[150] The police were ordered by Alabama's Governor George Wallace to "take whatever means were necessary" to prevent the march. When the police met the peaceful demonstrators, a blood bath of violence ensued with men, women, and children being indiscriminately bludgeoned by police. The first one attacked was John Robert Lewis. His skull was cracked opened by a state trooper's nightstick. When Lewis tried to get up, he was bludgeon in the head a second time. Afterwards, he lay unconscious on the concrete bridge. A fourteen-year-old girl needed thirty-five stitches to her skull after being severally attacked by troopers.[151] Police were attacking demonstrators with tear gas, bull whips, and rubber tubing wrapped in barbed wire as white spectators cheered with delight. Over fifty marchers were hospitalized including John Robert Lewis.

150   *H History*, "How Selma's 'Bloody Sunday' Became a Turning Point in the Civil Rights Movement" by Christopher Klein, July 18, 2020
151   *The Washington Post*, "John Lewis Nearly Died on the Edmund Pettus Bridge" / by Sidney Trent, 7/6/2020

I have lost all sense of fear, and when you lose all sense of fear, you are free.
John Robert Lewis

That horrible day in Selma is now referred to as "Bloody Sunday." Live coverage of the malicious attacks were seen by nearly fifty million television viewers across the United States.[152] Our nation's citizens were so outraged witnessing this senseless brutality that they joined the cause demanding that blacks be given equal rights at the voting booth. Over eighty demonstrations supporting the protesters took place throughout the United States the next few days. Two months later, President Lyndon Johnson signed the Voting Rights Act into law.

On several occasions, John Lewis knew he was probably going to be beaten by the police or by white thugs as he boldly went forward participating in civil-rights demonstrations. He knew this in 1961 as a Freedom Rider, for he was beaten unconscious at a Montgomery bus terminal and left lying in his own blood. He knew this as the leader crossing the Edmund Pettus Bridge, where he suffered a fractured skull. Between 1960 and 1965, Lewis was repeatedly assaulted by police and white demonstrators and arrested over forty times. He believed in a faith involving his own survivability, somehow knowing he would always endure his thrashings.

John Lewis was elected to Congress in 1986 representing Georgia's fifth district and served seventeen terms in the U.S. House of Representatives. After John Lewis was elected to Congress, he was arrested five more times as he continued his bold fight for the rights of others.

He remembers going to his farm where hundreds of chickens were enclosed in a fenced in area. He started talking to the chickens about important events of the day. The chickens all nodded, shaking their heads in approval indicating they understood what he was saying. Lewis stated he liked doing that because it appeared the chickens were paying more attention to his words than when he was speaking before members of Congress.[153]

When it became obvious that peaceful demonstrators would be injured or sent to jail for their participation in an event, occasionally they would opt out and not participate. Such was never the case with John. He always peacefully proceeded head-on into "good trouble," into "necessary

---

152 *H History*, "How Selma's 'Bloody Sunday' Became a Turning Point in the Civil Rights Movement" by Christopher Klein, July 18, 2020
153 "Good Trouble" video about John Robert Lewis, Nongola Pictures, AGC and TIME Studios, CNN Films 2020

trouble," demonstrating a courage and persistence unknown to most. [154]

John Robert Lewis died from pancreatic cancer on July 17, 2020. In a eulogy presented by the Speaker of the House, Nancy Pelosi, she referred to Lewis as "The Conscience of the Congress." Before dying, he left a message encouraging all those willing to pick up and continue his cause:

Though I may not be here with you, I urge you to answer the highest calling of your heart and stand up for what you truly believe. In my life I have done all I can to demonstrate the way of peace, the way of love and nonviolence is the more excellent way. Now it is your turn to let freedom ring.
John Robert Lewis

Perhaps John Robert Lewis, in his own way, was encouraging everyone "to get in the way, to get into good trouble, necessary trouble."

I celebrate the life and labors of John Robert Lewis as one of my heroes of peace because he frequently put his safety at risk for the benefits of others. Despite his many beatings from police, he was a true man of nonviolence never striking back.

Fury spends itself pretty quickly when there is no fury facing it.
John Robert Lewis

John Lewis preached and lived excellence and love in his life's endeavors. He openly and boldly fought for the rights and equality of all people: blacks, whites, women, and LGBTQ. "He was about civil rights, equality and liberation for everybody. Period. Full stop."[155]

Lewis at Comic-Con in San Diego

Comic-Cons are conventions where spectators and vendors dress up like Batman, Superman, the Hulk, and other super heroes found in comic books. In 2015, Lewis attended the San Diego Comic-Con to promote his book, *March*. He dressed up as himself crossing the Edmund Pettus Bridge wearing the same trench coat and backpack containing two books and a toothbrush. A group of elementary school children listened to Lewis

---

154 *New York Times. Nytimes.com*, by Katharine Q. Seelye, "John Lewis, Towering Figure of Human Rights Era, Dies at 80," July 17, 2020.
155 NBC News, nbcnews,com, Victoria Kirby York, National LGBTQ Task Force, commenting on Lewis after his death.

talk. To promote his book, *March*, Lewis decided to stage a march through the halls of Comic-Con with these kids. They all held hands and started marching. By the time Lewis reached the main show area, there were over 1,000 people holding hands and marching. Spectators, witnessing a real hero in an impromptu event of love, were near tears.[156]

"It was not enough," he would say, to simply endure a beating. It was not enough to resist the urge to strike back at an assailant. "That urge can't be there," he would tell us. "You have to do more than just not hit back. You have to have no desire to hit back. You have to love that person who is hitting you. You're going to love him."[157]

"John Lewis is the most courageous person I have ever met."
Representative James E. Clyburn (D-SC)

Closing thoughts

This book, as I went through its many revisions, used to be called *Without Regard to Consequences: Embodying the Values of Heroes of Peace*. The term, "Without Regard to Consequences" implied modern-day heroes of peace commit themselves to helping others regardless of the danger. When helping strangers in a crisis, we do weigh our danger and safety before getting involved. Many of us are responsible for the safety and wellbeing of families, children, and the elderly, and our safety is necessary to help these loved ones and provide for their future.

John Robert Lewis is one of few heroes on my chosen list that has always boldly moved forward "Without Regard to Consequences." He was severely injured and nearly killed several times as he peacefully fought for the rights of others. Such behavior indicates a dedication and sacrifice well beyond what is necessary to be a true hero of peace. It is a miracle that Lewis died from pancreatic cancer instead of from one of the many beatings he suffered from the police and white extremists.

You must be bold, brave, and courageous, and find a way…to get in the way.
John Robert Lewis

---

156 CNN Politics, *He dressed up at Comic-Con. He preached to chickens. He's the John Lewis you don't know*. By John Blake, July 18, 2020
157 *Walking with the Wind, A Memoir of the Movement*. John Robert Lewis. Simon and Schuster Paperbacks, New York 1998 Page 85 Jim Lawson instructing John Lewis and others in the art of nonviolence.

Never give up. Never give in. Never become hostile…
Hate is too big a burden to bear.
John Robert Lewis

I've seen courage in action on many occasions, but I can't say I've seen anyone
possess more of it and use it for any better purpose or to any greater
effect, than John Lewis.
Senator John McCain of Arizona

FRANK "THE FACILITATOR" HUEZO
FATHER MARCO DESSY
Amigos of Compassion—Rotary Assisted
Profession Father Marco Dessy: Missionary for the poor
Profession Frank "the Facilitator" Huezo: Import / Export Flowers and
child rescue coordinator
City and Country: Chinandega, Nicaragua
Compassionate endeavor: The rescue, education, and health care of
children living on the city of Chinandega's garbage dumps

Frank Huezo is a facilitator, a person who integrates a project's activities
to help insure a completion, a trouble shooter who can foresee and then
avoid future complications, and a locater and gatherer of effective resources
required for a quality outcome. When Frank's talents are applied to rescuing and educating children living on a city garbage dump, his positive
personality characteristics create enthusiasm in his workers, raise their energy levels, and promote harmony in volunteers for overcoming the many
obstacles encountered. When rescuing destitute children, Frank's inspiring
and recurring results are heartwarming and often bring participants and
observers to tears.

Nicaragua, the largest country in Central America, suffered through
a twelve-year revolution between 1978 and 1990 that bankrupted the
country and claimed 40,000 casualties. The resulting collapsed economy
took Nicaragua from a profitable tropical paradise to the second poorest
county in the western hemisphere—second only to Haiti.[158] The resulting

---

158 *Wikipedia*, Wikimedia/wiki/Nicaraguan_Revolution,

annual average income became less than $1.00 per day. Although primary school was free for children, many among the population could not afford the required shoes, uniforms, and school supplies; therefore, over 800,000 children did not attend school.

Father Marco Dessy, an Italian missionary serving the poor in Chinandega, Nicaragua, discovered over 800 children—some three-years-old or younger—living in squalor on the Chinandega City garbage dump. These nearly naked children were victims of the horrific poverty continuing to spread from the economic collapse generated by Nicaraguan Revolution. Covered with infected open sores and hundreds of flies, these children ran after garbage trucks arriving at the dump trying to be the first to search through their spoils. Each child carried a long stick used to prod through the contaminated refuse. Many loose cattle, horses, and dogs aimlessly roamed the dump competing with the children for scraps of rotted food. Any oranges that were found were revered, for although their outer skin was covered in green mold, at times this contamination did not completely penetrate to the inner fruit.

The beginning of the School of the Dump

In 1995, Father Dessy built the Children of the Dump School next to the Chinandega city dump from donations raised from several sources. The initial school was a two-room building. Children from the dump who attended this school were given one hot and nutritious lunch per day as an incentive to keep going to class. No attendance in class, no hot lunch. Initially, ninety children from the dump joined the school.

Fourteen of these desperate children at Father Dessy's rescue mission were blind. Transportation for these blind children was not available and was severely needed to visit doctors and medical centers. In 1997, Father Dessy continued his donor grapevine in hopes of finding people who could donate something toward a small bus. His pleas found their way into Rotary Clubs in Southern Texas, to be specific, the Humble Rotary Club. Frank Huezo, a member of the Club, served as the facilitator for the bus project.

Frank was born, raised, educated, married, and had his first child in Nicaragua. It is where his heart belongs. In 1979, during the ordeal of the Nicaraguan revolution, Frank, with his daughter Maria and his wife, Mary, pregnant with their second child, decided to move to Houston, Texas, and start a new life.

The story of the Children of the Dump touched Frank deeply, so he started raising money through his friends and associates until a small bus

was purchased and shipped to Father Marco Dessy in December 1996. Two months later, Frank flew to Chinandega and checked on the new bus, met Father Marco Dessy, and visited the Chinandega garbage dump viewing 800 grimy children, partially clothed in torn and soiled rags, scavenging through rotten garbage for food. Frank was quoted in a newspaper, "It looked like a war zone! It was the worst type of human drama that anyone could see!"

Starving and homeless children in a broken economy ravaged by civil war—could it get any worse?

Yes, it did get worse. On October 22, 1998, Category-5 Hurricane Mitch, with peak winds of 180 mph (285 km/h), slowly crept its way onto Nicaragua like a colossal monster—and there it sat for ten days steadily chewing and gnawing on everything in its path as it swept the landscape clean. Mitch was the most powerful hurricane to hit Nicaragua since the Great Hurricane of 1780.

Many homes in Nicaragua are little more than tin shacks or plastic tarps tied together between trees. Hurricane Mitch devastated such vulnerable structures with ease killing 3,800 people. A continuous torrential five-day rain filled the Casitas Volcano crater in northwestern Nicaragua mixing it with lava until the crater's wall fractured creating a mudslide that buried four little villages at the volcano's base in mud and debris.[159] When the mudslide stopped, schools, homes, and churches were buried, children were screaming for help clutching the branches of uprooted trees, and others were crying for help half buried in the quick-sand type sludge. Survivors outside the mud attempted to rescue those close enough to grab a thrown rope and be pulled to safety. Many were buried up to their necks. Most were too far away to grab a thrown rope, including the children clinging to the uprooted trees. There

---

159 *Los Angeles Times, Site of Nicaragua Mudslide Becomes National Cemetery*, by Juanita Darling, November 5, 1998

were many dead bodies throughout the area and many, still unidentified, were burned by survivors to prevent area contamination.

It continued to rain for days after Mitch slowly crawled out of the area. The Casitas Volcano's thirst seemed unquenchable as its crater again filled with rain. Three days later, a second mud slide roared from the volcano's fractured crown devastating much of the surviving parts of the four villages. Most of the uprooted trees, still harboring frantic children interwoven in their branches, were swept away. Thousands of people were killed as the second mud slide ravaged its way to the northwestern province of Chinandega.

During the following days, Army rescue efforts pulled about 360 bodies from the mud. The four villages formally housed an estimated 2,000 people; only ninety-two were found alive.[160]

The killer winds of Hurricane Mitch, the associated mass flooding, and the Casitas Volcano mud slides destroyed thousands of homes, leaving nearly 20% of Nicaragua's population homeless.

Thousands of displaced survivors, without food, water, shelter, or medical aid, desperately searched the countryside for any type of refuge. Some found sanctuary in city garbage dumps. They looked for food amid the rotting refuse. Others found relative safety in deep ravines where a source of contaminated water offered them some small hope.

Father Dessy reached out in desperation to his former donors, to NGOs (non-government organizations), to his friends and business acquaintances, to the American Red Cross, to Doctors without Borders, and to Amigos in Christ. Father Dessy and his crisis organization then served over 47,000 located refugees from October 1998 through February of 1999. They consisted of the homeless, the abandoned, the squatters and refugees, the school students, and those restricted to hospitals.[161]

Over 2,800 hurricane Mitch refugees found their way to the Chinandega City Dump joining the 800 children found there by Father Dessy. The Mayor of Chinandega owned the property next to the city dump. This land was where most of the 2,800 people became squatters making shacks from discarded material found on the garbage dump. This land, however, had no water, and it was below the neighboring sanitary sewer plant for Chinandega. Every time heavy rain was experienced, raw human waste would flow down from the sewage plant and flood the squatter's makeshift shacks with human excrement. This was deplorable. Another area had to be located for the impoverished trying to cling to life in this filthy place.

---

160 *Independent News*, "Nearly 3,000 dead missing as hurricane devastates Nicaragua" by Phil Davison, 11/2/1998
161 Told to the author by Frank Huezo in October 2020.

Frank Huezo and several of his associates realized that an organization was needed to coordinate and promote the many Children of the Dump projects to Rotary Clubs in Central America and the United States. In 1999, they formed Hope and Relief International Inc. to satisfy this need. Forming this organization became a major project of the Humble Club in Texas.

Building communities offering sustainability

Frank Huezo and Father Marco Dessy knew if you feed the poor, you will be feeding them forever. It was necessary to make them independent with the ability to clothe, feed, and educate themselves. With this in mind, land located eight miles south of Chinandega, that was formerly used for raising sugar cane and peanuts, was donated by a friend of Father Marco Dessy. On this land, a school and 325 houses were built, and each lot included fruit trees, vegetable gardens, chickens, a rooster, and a pig. Squatters living in the dump area below the sewer plant were moved to this new development. It was named Sainte Matilde and became the model program for Hope and Relief International.

I was a member of the Aurora Rotary Club in Ohio and started receiving fliers about Saint Matilde and the wonderful sustainability factor associated with the program. I had not met Frank yet, but I was influenced by his promotional hard work. My Aurora Rotary Club started fund-raising projects for Sainte Matilde. In 2000, I attended a Rotary governor's conference in Niagara Falls. One of the programs associated with this conference was through a man named Frank Huezo speaking about the Children of the Dump in Chinandega, Nicaragua. Frank, the "facilitator" was hard at work thousands of miles away from Chinandega spreading the word and raising funds. This was where I met Frank and learned more about the Children of the Dump.

Searching continued in Nicaragua to locate more destitute people ravaged by the poor economy and hurricanes. Thirty-seven families were found living in a ravine near the little village of Saint Pablo. Father Dessy asked Frank for help starting a program through Hope and Relief International to build them their own village. Masons and carpenters were brought in to train the people living in the ravine so they could build their own houses. Having built their house, they would have the knowledge and ability to maintain it. All the workers took part in building a school. Those who worked the hardest were given a deed to their own house; those who did not work were left without. Only women were deeded a house, for they had children and felt obligated to be more responsible than the men who had a habit of disappearing over weekends. It was requested by the new villagers to name the housing complex Rotary Village in appreciation for all the Rotary Clubs that contributed their time and money.

Trips to Nicaragua for awareness and fund raising

For over twenty years, Frank has been escorting Nicaraguan tours three times per year to Rotarians and other interested parties involving the many Children of the Dump projects. I joined one of these tours and visited the dump, the Children-of-the-Dump school, Sainte Matilde, and was present at Rotary Village upon its completion when the deeds to the houses were awarded to the hard-working women who built them. These guided trips also increased awareness of the poor, encouraged fund-raising, and allowed donors to take a personal look at the results of their philanthropic endeavors.

Many children from the dump who had graduated from high school also wanted to attend college. These trips to Nicaragua guided by Frank also provided opportunities for participants to sponsor high school graduates at a local college.

Several blind children were living at a special facility built in 1977. One of them was named Chilo, a blind girl with a beautiful singing voice. She graduated first in her class from high school, not a special school for the blind. She went on to finish college earning a degree in psychology. She is now working for the Chinandega 2001 Foundation as a psychologist serving blind children living on the Chinandega City dump.

Maria Joze Perez Lopez was taken off the dump when she was ten years old. She graduated from high school and then attended college.

After graduating from college, she perused graduate school and earned an M.B.A. (Master of Business Administration). She now owns her own restaurant and volunteers helping the children from the dump at their many facilities. In this photo, Frank addresses a group of prospective donors with Maria Jose standing by.

A vocational high school

Father Dessy's promotional efforts were starting to get international attention from the King and Queen of Spain. To give the children of the Dump students an advantage after graduation in finding employment, the Spanish government built a high school that trained students in occupational endeavors as well as the required high school subjects. The Batania Trade School, finished in the year 2000, educates students in metallurgy, welding, wood working, confectionery sugar candy production, and sewing and making clothing. During my four trips with Frank to Nicaragua, I witnessed children from the dump making chairs and tables, church pews, doors, and intricate hard-wood carvings. A professionally manufactured Rotary dress shirt was purchased and given to the children who were learning sewing. The next day they had duplicated the shirt with one of higher quality. I could not believe my eyes.

A special home for expectant mothers

Expectant young girls in Nicaragua are frequently around fourteen to sixteen years old, poor, living in remote mountain villages, and without transportation or medical treatment. A caring facility was urgently needed. A perfect house for this purpose was for sale for $35,000, but where could such funds be located? A friend of Father Dessy living in Italy donated a Rolex President watch toward the project. It sold for $23,000. The rest of the money resulted from a national fund raiser drive among Rotary Clubs. On three separate occasions, I was given a tour of this special facility and had an opportunity to meet and converse with the wonderful people within the home. Some of the expectant mothers had walked over 50 miles, alone, from their mountain village to get to this loving port-in-the-storm.

A fully operational hospital

In 2001, a $200,000 gift was received from a donor in Atlanta, Georgia to build a hospital for the Children of the Dump and people of the surrounding area. Frank used his Rotary Club network to raise money for the hospital furnishings. Operating tables, wheel chairs, EKGs, x-ray machines, blood pressure monitors, and other customary hospital equipment were provided by many Rotary Clubs throughout the United States.

An organization was formed to solicit and coordinate medical brigades from around the globe. These brigades consist of teams of doctors, nurses, and other technical people who volunteer their time to come to the hospital in Nicaragua and perform operations for the poor. Surgical teams from the United States, France, Canada, and other areas arrive on the average about three times per year. They have performed thousands of operations saving untold lives.

What happened to the School of the Dump's two-room school house?

The School of the Dump grew to consist of several buildings, over thirty-five classrooms, a library, a music classroom, a computer training center, an athletic field, a kitchen, and dining hall. Perhaps the most moving item at the school is a graduation roster consisting of thousands of children removed from the Chinandega City dump and sent to school. What a success story.

The Getsemani Choir

Father Marco Dessy formed the Getsemani Choir. It consisted of around ten kids from the dump who sounded like angles when singing accompanied by a choir director and some dancers. The choir was taken on eight tours around the United States raising money to help support the Children of the Dump and other projects.

The choir toured from 1997 through 2005 giving performances in Atlanta, New York, New Orleans, Houston, Dallas, Michigan, and Connecticut. The first year they raised $47,000, the second year their revenue was $83,000, and such good fortune in fund raising followed the choir through 2005. The money was used to help build and support: the fishing Village of El Minco, the Batania Trade School, the new hospital, the home for pregnant women, and the School of the Dump.

While touring in New York on September 11, 2001, the choir was invited to sing for the United Nations. While driving to the United Nations to perform, a hijacked passenger jet flew into one of the towers at the World Trade Center. The United States had just been attacked by terrorists. The choir was canceled.

Do you believe in miracles?

Ludwig Vanegas and his brother Alex Vanegas were two children taken off the dump and raised by Father Marco Dessy. Both became guitar players, with Ludwig becoming the choir director.

Frank Huezo had a friend, Alonso Lacaya, dying of leukemia. This friend was in the hospice wing of the Herman Hospital. Frank, the choir, and Ludwick and Alex with their guitars, visited him on his death bed at 7:00 p.m. The choir and Frank wanted to say goodbye before Alonso died. Ludwick and Alex started playing their guitars accompanied by the choir who broke into song singing "Jesus Is Here." Quickly, doctors and nurses rushed to the area requesting quiet for the rest of the patients. Within a few minutes, however, the doctors and nurses were dancing, clapping their hands, and singing along showing great enthusiasm. It turned into a gala party.

The next morning at 10:00 a.m., Alonso Lacaya tested clean for cancer. Two days later he left the hospital and went home.[162]

In December of 2007, I was in Nicaragua with Frank Huezo and nine students from Hiram College. I was teaching a class on child poverty and using the children of the dump as a resource. My fiancé, Carol Ruggie, was in hospice back in Ohio dying of pancreatic cancer. Visiting us at our hotel that night was Alex Ludwick and a member of the choir who sang "Jesus Is Here" to Frank's friend. I am not saying that I believe in miracles, but I asked if they would sing over the phone to Carol Ruggie in her hospice bed in Ohio. They agreed. I called Carol on her cell phone. Her voice was very weak and shaky. I tried to explain to Carol what was about to happen, and I think she understood. The singing and guitar playing was beautiful. I cried during this experience. It was wonderful; however, the results were not the same. Carol died on December 13, 2007.

Carol was not only involved with the Children-of-the-Dump, but also involved with Sparrow Village in South Africa, a village for children dying of AIDS (see the section on Reverend Corrine, p. 156). Carol was cremated, and the following year I took her ashes to South Africa and sprinkled half of them around Sparrow Village. I then went on another mission tour in Nicaragua and sprinkled the other half of Carol's ashes around the School of the Dump. Carol's remains are now surrounded by the children she loved.

I told Frank that I was writing a book about special heroes of peace, and I wanted to include him in my book as an example for others to follow. Frank modestly stated, "I'm just a facilitator, Roger, I'm far short of a hero." I thought to myself, "That's what all heroes of peace say."

---

162 As reported to me by Frank Huezo

"Well," I said to Frank, "According to my sources, you have helped facilitate quite a lot!" And I listed these accomplishments:

- the health and wellbeing of over 25,000 pregnant women and their new born children through the Home for Expectant Mothers
- the rescue, nourishment, safety, and education of over 20,000 children living on the Chinandega garbage dump
- the education and job training for thousands of children on the dump through the Batania Trade School
- the coordination and participation of hundreds of volunteers in helping the poor
- the collection of millions of dollars for the Children-of-the-Dump projects
- the rescue of thousands of refugees from poverty, revolution, and natural disasters
- thousands of medical operations for the poor through the hospital you help furnish and maintain
- the installations of many water wells, wash basins, and latrines in several Nicaraguan villages

Frank continues to promote awareness and raise money for these hungry children. He has conducted over sixty trips to Chinandega from the United States and escorted more than 1,200 people into his special world of compassion for these wonderful, desperate kids. I am one of those 1200 people.

Frank, Father Marco Dessy, and other managerial volunteers raised funds for the projects mention through many Rotary Clubs, the Chinandega 2001 Foundation, Amigos for Christ, the American Red Cross, Doctors Without Borders, the Getsemani Choir tours, and private donors to name a few.

Closing thought

Glenys van Halter learned that there were thousands of small children near her home who had no school to attend and were routinely sexually molested during the day. She did something about it. She discovered that nine-year-old girls were working as prostitutes so they could raise some money for food. Glenys started a trade school for the girls to get them off the streets.

Olga Sanchez learned that thousands of people were trying to escape violence and oppression from Central America and Mexico by hanging on to a freight train day and night. She learned many of these desperate people lost their arms and legs when falling off the train during their escape. She would walk the tracks looking for their severed limbs and their remaining torsos in a desperate attempt to save them. She then sold cookies and bread and sought donations to purchase over 2,500 prosthetic limbs for these distressed people.

Frank Huezo spent the over twenty-five years coordinating the means to feed, house, and educate thousands of children living on a garbage dump in Nicaragua. Many of these children finished high school while other earned college degrees. Without Frank, they would be scavenging for life on a garbage dump and praying that the rotten orange they just found was not decayed inside.

Where do we find such people? They frequently find us. It is critical to understand what the efforts of one person guiding others can accomplish. This realization helps build our confidence and offers examples of the nearly unlimited potential of being human.

Why did you read this book?

We have finally come to that question. I assume that many readers have undertaken this manuscript to learn about wonderful heroic endeavors accomplished by truly inspiring people. Such stories fill our hearts with wonderment. Others may have read this book to possibly try and adapt some of these wonderful values into their character. If so, I have good news. Many readers already possess several of the heroes' fourteen values, some already give anonymously, while other readers are masters of intentional free choice.

Between stimulus and response there is a space. In that space is our power to choose our response. In our response lies our growth and our freedom.
Viktor E. Frankl

KEY POINT

*One wonderful epiphany of my research was to realize that one of the
fourteen values connects the other thirteen. I observed that all eighty
of my specially chosen heroes of peace accomplished all fourteen values
in their loving endeavors by practicing only one, and as they did so, the
other thirteen fell into place. I greatly feared that it would be a most
daunting task for me to eventually behave with the kindness and love
of my selected eighty heroes of peace—for me to master all fourteen
values. I surely would have to study, practice, and learn all these values
until they became second nature to me. But my inspiring eighty heroes of
peace showed me that I had to master but one value of peace: Preserving
character.*

*Our heroes of peace typically react to whatever happens to them
with calm kindness, understanding, and compassion. This automatically
fulfills the wonderful values of choosing their most effective behavior,
of creating the most positive change, of developing the most optimistic
vision, and of eagerly confronting all obstacles with a confident attitude. These heroes know that such optimism coupled with love will insure
their self-esteem, display their compassion for all to see, bring their
courage forward to guide their decisions, and allow perseverance to be
the master at their helm. Reacting with kindness, understanding, and
compassion will certainly instill trust, insure peaceful outcomes when
managing conflict, prevent unfair and prejudicial judgments, encourage
recognition for other's achievements, and, most importantly, preserve
and revere these values for the enrichment of themselves and others.*

*"Mother Teresa's inner peace and happiness did not depend on external
acquisitions, but how she personally responded to circumstances and
situations. . . . It is not necessarily dependent on what happens, but on
how you respond to the circumstance that life presents you."*[163]

---

163   Paul A Wright, Cardiologist—*Mother Teresa's Prescription, Finding Happiness and Peace in
Service*, ava maria press, Notre Dame, Indiana, Page 42, 2006

I have shared with you the wonderful significance and capabilities of being human. I studied incredibly loving people, explored their hearts, and rode the waves of optimism in their dreams. I researched these heroes of peace on their rescues of the destitute, on their quests to calm injustices, on their missions of peace addressing the perils of discrimination, and when they forged ahead where obstacles are cherished as opportunities for growth.

Heroes of peace understand that fear offers them the only opportunity they will ever have to demonstrate courage; therefore, they respect fear and welcome it as an occasional visitor at their door. They understand how their self-esteem must only be determined by themselves, never giving others the power to control such a vital entity. They realize that their failures are actually successfully completed steppingstones to their goal, and they understand that their continuous examples of excellence serve as a beacon for others to follow. Heroes of peace do not have a need to always be right, they know that the most important part of any conflict is maintaining the dignity of their adversaries, and they realize that the best type of giving requires no recognition or reward. They seek the differences in others and celebrated them for their enrichment, they do not use them to diminish, degrade, or segregate. Heroes of peace search for those unable to speak for themselves and represent them through life's challenges. And most important of all, how heroes of peace react to people and circumstances determines their character; it determines for all to see who they really are.

When you march into hell for a heavenly cause, you will not have much company, but any company you do have will be magnificent!
Roger F. Cram

Revering these Values

Uphold this Value System, especially under adverse conditions, not to please someone else, but to honor the unfaltering principles within you, to validate your character as the type of person you want to be, and to gradually realize the awesome potential of being human.

Be more concerned with your character than your reputation, because your character is who you really are while your reputation is simply what others think you are.
Unknown

Reputation is the shadow. Character is the tree.
Abraham Lincoln

One can easily judge the character of a person by the way they treat people who can do nothing for them.
Proverb

Final thoughts

I have not ended this book with a triumphant, life-changing epiphany. I have ended this book with a quiet whisper of peace, with a calm notion to encourage compassion and kindness, with hope that we all embrace the serenity living within our hearts, and with a quiet prayer for us to realize just how magnificent we can become.

The End

(Or hopefully, the beginning)

Dear Reader:

I thank you for sharing my wonderful journey as we voyaged through this book together. I enjoyed your companionship. I am grateful for your interest in peaceful heroes and the compassionate magic that dwells in their hearts.

You are the only you that will ever exist. There will never be another. Stay at your helm. The world will be enriched because you are here.

Most Respectfully,

Roger F. Cram

Appendix

Some of the programs I presented about the Tuskegee Airmen

- The Tuskegee Airmen's Celebration, November 2003, Hiram College, Hiram, Ohio
- The Tuskegee Women's Banquet, November 20, 2004, Hiram College, Hiram, Ohio
- The Tuskegee Airmen National Convention in August 2005 at Orlando, Florida
- The Black Military Heroes Banquet, November 2005, the Tuskegee Airmen, the 761st Tank Battalion, the Triple Nickels Parachute Team, the USS Mason, and the Red Ball Express – Hiram College, Hiram, Ohio in 2006
- Discovering Heroic Values, three-day seminar, Winnipeg, Manitoba, Canada. August 2006
- The Tuskegee University in Tuskegee, Alabama, in March of 2006
- The Cleveland School Board – March 19, 2007
- Movie World Premiere—Flying for Freedom—Untold Stories of the Tuskegee Airmen—Dallas, Texas—November 14, 2007
- The Tuskegee Airmen National Convention in Gaylord, Texas on August 21, 2007
- American Heritage Committee, Travis Air Force Base in California, February 19, 2008
- The Lee Archer Chapter of the Tuskegee Airmen at Travis Air Force Base in California on November 8, 2008
- The Department of Defense, Joint Force Headquarters—Air Force Reserve in Washington D.C.
- The 110th Fighter Wing in Battle Creek, Michigan, February 24, 2009
- The Tuskegee Airmen National Convention in Philadelphia, Pennsylvania on July 17, 2008
- The United States Naval Reserve in Cleveland, Ohio in 2008
- The Scott Air Force Base Belleville, Illinois, February 8, 2008
- The United States Army Reserve in Saint Louis, Missouri
- The United States Air Force Reserve Youth Week—students from Selfridge, Michigan Air Force Base, held at the Akron-Canton Airport in Akron, Ohio.
- North Coast Chapter of the Tuskegee Airmen—2008 Summer Youth Camp (Three one-week programs)—Burke Lakefront Airport, Cleveland, Ohio.

- The dedication of the restoration and grand opening of Molton Field by the National Park Service in Tuskegee, Alabama, on October 4, 2008.
- The United States Coast Guard in Camp Perry, Ohio
- The 615th Contingency Response Wing at Travis Air Force Base in California on January 24, 2009
- The United States Air Force Reserve in Cleveland, Ohio, in 2009
- The Youth Recognition Ceremony at the Tuskegee Airmen National Convention in Las Vegas, Nevada on August 6, 2009
- The African American Heritage Culmination Dinner, February 25, 2010, Club Five Six, 56th Fighter Wing F-16 fighter jet training at Luke Air Force Base, Phoenix, Arizona
- The City Club of Cleveland 100th Anniversary, October 29, 2010

Some interesting statistics about the Tuskegee Airmen

- 994 pilots graduated from Tuskegee.
- 450 pilots were sent overseas.
  75 died fighting for their country.
- The Tuskegee Airmen's 332nd Fighter Group flew 311 missions
- 179 missions were bomber escort
- 132 missions were tactical ground targets
- During the 179 bomber-escort missions, they escorted 15,533 bombers. This averages 87 bombers escorted per mission.
- Of the 179 bomber-escort missions, 33 of these missions encountered German fighter planes
- At an average of 87 bombers per mission, 33 missions x 87 = about 2,863 bombers were escorted when the Tuskegee Airmen encountered German fighter planes.
- During these 33 missions, seven bombers were shot down by German fighters.
- Seven bombers out of 2,863 = .24% (1/4th of one percent of the escorted bombers were shot down!)

Source: *Eleven Myths about the Tuskegee Airmen* by Daniel Haulman New South Books, Montgomery, Alabama 2012.

**The Shared Characteristics of Peace from
My Eighty Selected Heroes**

True heroes of peace…

- Know that how they react to any person or incident determines their true character and boldly announces to all who they are—the most important value.
- Care for themselves in all areas, forgive themselves, and are gentle and kind with themselves, knowing they are the only ones who can do so; stay calm and think clearly while experiencing threats, conflict, or a crisis.
- Govern themselves by never allowing another's bad behavior to negatively influence their conduct.
- Encourage positive change, not through criticism, but through their continuous achievements of excellence for all to witness.
- Envision things as wonderful as they can be, not as they are, and then strive to create positive change toward these envisioned goals.
- Realize that obstacles are not barriers to their goals, but opportunities for growth and the challenge to learn new skills.
- Enhance their self-esteem, not from the opinions of others, but from the compassionate causes they have embraced and the perseverance and courage they expended toward their resolve.
- Give simply to increase the amount of goodness in the world—often without recognition or reward.
- Honor and respect fear, for fear alone offers them an opportunity to show courage.
- Never give up. The only time they can fail is if they quit pursuing their goals.
- Honor all commitments and obligations to everyone, especially themselves. Their pledge should be as meaningful to a beggar as to a king.
- Always maintain the dignity of their adversaries.
- Observe, but never judge. They seek out the differences in others and then celebrate them, for such diversity is the true potpourri of humanity and will enrich them with the knowledge and wisdom of the human experience.
- Serve enthusiastically as a spokesperson for the accomplishments and concerns of others.

- Uphold their own values, especially under adverse conditions—not to please someone else, but to honor their own unfaltering principles and validate their character as the type of person they want to be—and to gradually realize the awesome potential of being human.
- Do not have a need to be right.
- Feel it is their responsibility and obligation as a human being to care for those less fortunate—as only humans can do.
- Solve problems peacefully, beneficial to all concerned: win-win.
- Should always be at peace even though their surroundings are chaotic.

My Eighty Chosen Heroes of Peace

42 males, 38 females, 43 Countries

(Number to the left of a name indicates the page number when a hero is discussed in detail in this book)

Countries or areas my heroes represent in alphabetical order
Austria, Bosnia, Burundi, Burma, Cameroon, Cambodia, Canada, the Caribbean, Chechnya, Dominican Republic, El Salvador, England, France, Germany, Ghana, Guatemala, Guinea, Haiti, India, Indonesia, Iran, Kenya, Liberia, Mali, Malawi, Mexico, Mongolia, Nepal, Nicaragua, Pakistan, Peru, Philippines, Romania, Russia, Scotland, Senegal, Sierra Leone, South Africa, Tanzania, the United States, and Zimbabwe.

Page #	Hero's Name	Country	Humanitarian Cause
	Susan B. Anthony	USA	Women's rights & equality
	Khassan Baiev	Chechnya	Surgeon for children of War Caring for Children of War
	Kevin Bales	USA, worldwide	Human trafficking abolitionist, educator, author
	Linda Bergendahl-Pauling	USA	Make-A-Wish Foundation— terminally ill kids
	Susan Burton	USA	Support for ex-cons, community crusader
	Jimmy Carter	USA, worldwide	World health
	George Washington Carver	USA	Poor farmers—education, crop rotation
	César Estrada Chávez	USA	Rights of migrant workers
100	Principal Daniels Crime and the Poor	South Africa	Youth education, crime, poor children
31	Benjamin O. Davis Jr.	USA	Representing Tuskegee Airmen, racial equality
	Maggie Dayne	Nepal	Caring for women and children
	Brisa De Angulo	Bolivia	Advocates against child abuse
186	Father Marco Dessy	Nicaragua	Rescue/educate children from the dump
	Sal Dimisali	USA	Hero to the poor
173	Gilbert Doho	Cameroon	Teaching human rights through theater
	Shirin Ebadi	Iran	Rights of women, children, and refugees
	Albert Einstein	USA	Physicist/humanitarian
	Paul Farmer	USA, Caribbean	Medical standards and relief for the poor
143	Flower Man	South Africa	Entrepreneur for the poor
	Victor E. Frankl	Austria	Existential analysis, living through hardships

ge #

	Tina Frundt	USA	Rescuer of sex slaves
	Ganbayasgakh Geleg	Mongolia	Preventing child trafficking
27	Mahatmha Gandhi	India	Human rights and equality
	Leymah Gbowee	Liberia	Women's rights
	Laura Germino	USA	Slavery migrant farm workers
	Andrew Greene Jr.	Sierra Leone	Teacher-iEARN, human rights, children of war
	Dr. Joe Greer	USA	Health care for the poor
132	Glenys van Halter	South Africa	Education for the poor
96	Paul Harris	USA, Worldwide	Founder Rotary International, world assistance
	Paul David "Bono" Hewson	Europe, Africa	AIDS and debt relief to poor nations, refugees
186	Frank Huezo	Nicaragua	Food/Education for children on city dump
112	Ryan Hreljac	Canada, worldwide	Water wells for the poor
	Nkosi Johnson	South Africa	Equality with AIDS
	William Kamkwamba	Malawi	Education and entrepreneurship for the poor
	Saddharth Kara	India, Africa	Fighting human trafficking and sex slavery
	Dr. Martin Luther King Jr.	USA	Human rights
	Anuradha Koirala	Nepal	Helping human trafficking victims
140	Claw Lady	South Africa	Caring for orphans of HIV AIDS
180	John Robert Lewis	USA	U. S. Congressman, Human rights
7	Abraham Lincoln	USA	Against slavery
	Robin Lynn	Indonesia	Birthing for the poor
	Wangari Maathai	Kenya	Restoring the devastation of Governments
	Magnus MacFarlane-Barrow	Scotland, Bosnia	Feeding children in refugee camps
86	Nelson Mandela	South Africa	Human rights
53	Masalakulangwa Mabula	Tanzania	Rescuing street children
	Iqbal Masih	Pakistan	Child slave labor carpet industry
	Liz McCartney	USA	Disaster recovery
56	Rev. Corine McClintock	South Africa	Home, food, shelter for children with AIDS
	Molly Melching	Senegal, Sudan, Mali, and Guinea	Female human rights
	Rigoberta Menchu	Guatemala	Human rights
	Florence Nightingale	England	Human rights and health care for the military

Page #

	Phymean Noun	Cambodia	Children of the dump
164	Dr. Meena Patel	USA, India	Human rights, caring for the destitute
	Gerson A. F. Perez	Columbia	Lands mine removal
113	Efren Peñaflorida	Philippines	Portable classrooms for poor children
	Sonia Pierre	Dominican Republic, Haiti	Human Rights for Haitian Girls
	Isabelle Redford	USA	Homes for orphans
119	Hal Reichle	USA	Anonymous Acts of kindness
	Archbishop Oscar Romero	El Salvador	Martyr for the Poor
34	Eleanor Roosevelt	USA	Human equality
	Christine Sabiyumva	Burundi	Child Trafficking Rescue
22	Ginetta Sagan	Germany	Release of Political Prisoners
177	Olga Sanchez	Mexico	Caring for Injured Refugees
40	Albert Schweitzer	Germany, France	Theologian, physician, author, philosopher, humanitarian
	Alexandria Scott	USA	Fund Raising for Cancer
149	Irena Sendler	Germany	Rescuing Children from the Nazis
	Lady Diana Spencer	England	Human rights and dignity for poor children
	Khali Sweeney	USA	Mentoring Street Children
109	Hannah Taylor	Canada	Caring for the homeless
19	Mother Teresa	India, Mexico	Caring for the wretched poor
	Harriet Tubman	USA	Helping slaves escape to freedom
22	Desmond Mpilo Tutu	South Africa	Human rights reconciliation
23	Booker T. Washington	USA	Civil rights and education
	Patty Webster	USA, Peru	Amazon Basin health care and education
	William Wilberforce	England	Ending slavery
	Jody Williams	El Salvador	Landmine removal & children's artificial limbs
	Amy Wright	USA	Employment for the Disabled
	Emmanuel Ofosu Yeboah	Ghana	Rights of the Handicapped
	Malala Yousafzai	Pakistan	Education for girls
	Muhammad Yunus	India	Banker to the Poor

CPSIA information can be obtained
at www.ICGtesting.com
Printed in the USA
LVHW030747020223
738080LV00002B/10